Amazing Dogs Lover Coloring Book
Small & Medium Size Dogs
Volume 2

Grayscale/Pencils Sketch Drawing from Photos

Illustrated by

Terry Luckado Fulgham

Copyright © 2020 Terry Luckado Fulgham
All rights reserved.

ISBN: 9781655754166
Imprint: Independently published

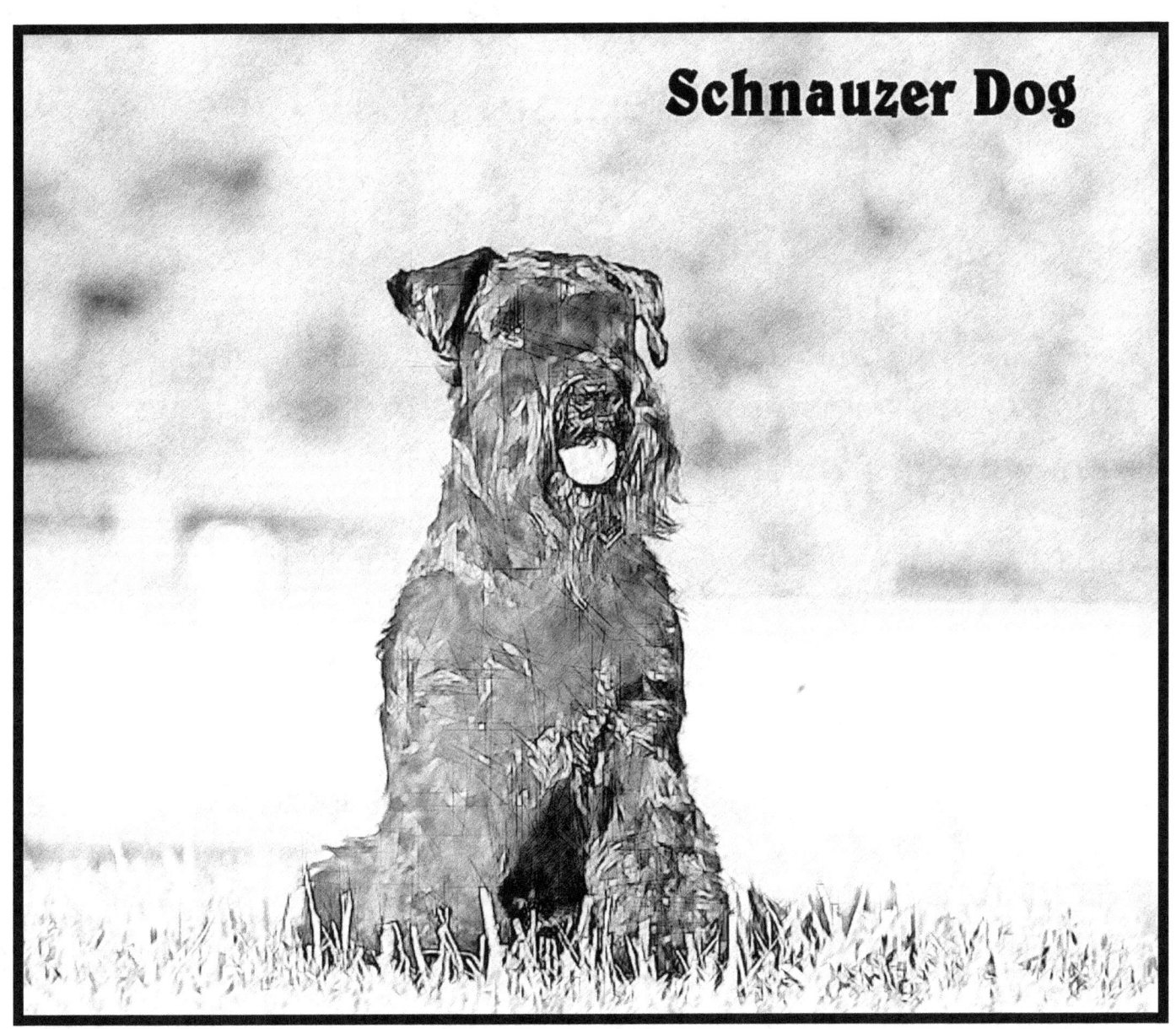

INTRODUCTION

Amazing Dogs Lover Coloring Book
Small & Medium Size Dogs
Volume 2

This coloring book is for children, girls and boys, teenagers & grownups - alike!

It can be fun for anyone who loves to color.

One image per page so you can color with pencils, pens, markers as you wish.

50 Amazingly Dog Breed Sketch's

Grayscale/Pencils Sketch Drawing from Photos.

This Amazing Dog Lover Coloring Book Large Breed Volume – 1 will keep you relaxed and calm, create artistic pictures you can tear out and hang around the house.

This book can be a practice book, for painters, artists, water colorists, teenagers and adults who love to color.

Use the richly hand drawn pencil sketch's in this book to produce your own works of art.
Thinking carefully about your color scheme will give your pictures harmony.

Inside this coloring book are 50 unique "pencil sketches" made from photos.

These actual photos are so richly drawn that after you are finished coloring you will have a lovely work of art worthy to be displayed on a wall.

You don't need the skills of a sketch artist to personalize these beautiful drawing.

Instantaneously start to reduce you stress level with your vision of each of these sketch.

HAPPY COLORING!!!

I hope you enjoy

Amazing Dogs Lover Coloring Book
Small & Medium Size Dogs
Volume 2

The images are printed on a single side of the paper to help prevent bleed-through.

We recommend putting a sheet of paper or card between pages if using strong inks.

Each page is marked with a cutting line to aid removal of pictures.

Sit back relax and bring the artistic and vibrant beauty of these many Amazing Dog Breeds to life through coloring.

Amazing Dogs Lover Coloring Book
Small & Medium Size Dogs
Volume 2

Grayscale/Pencils Sketch Drawing from Photos.

This book belongs to

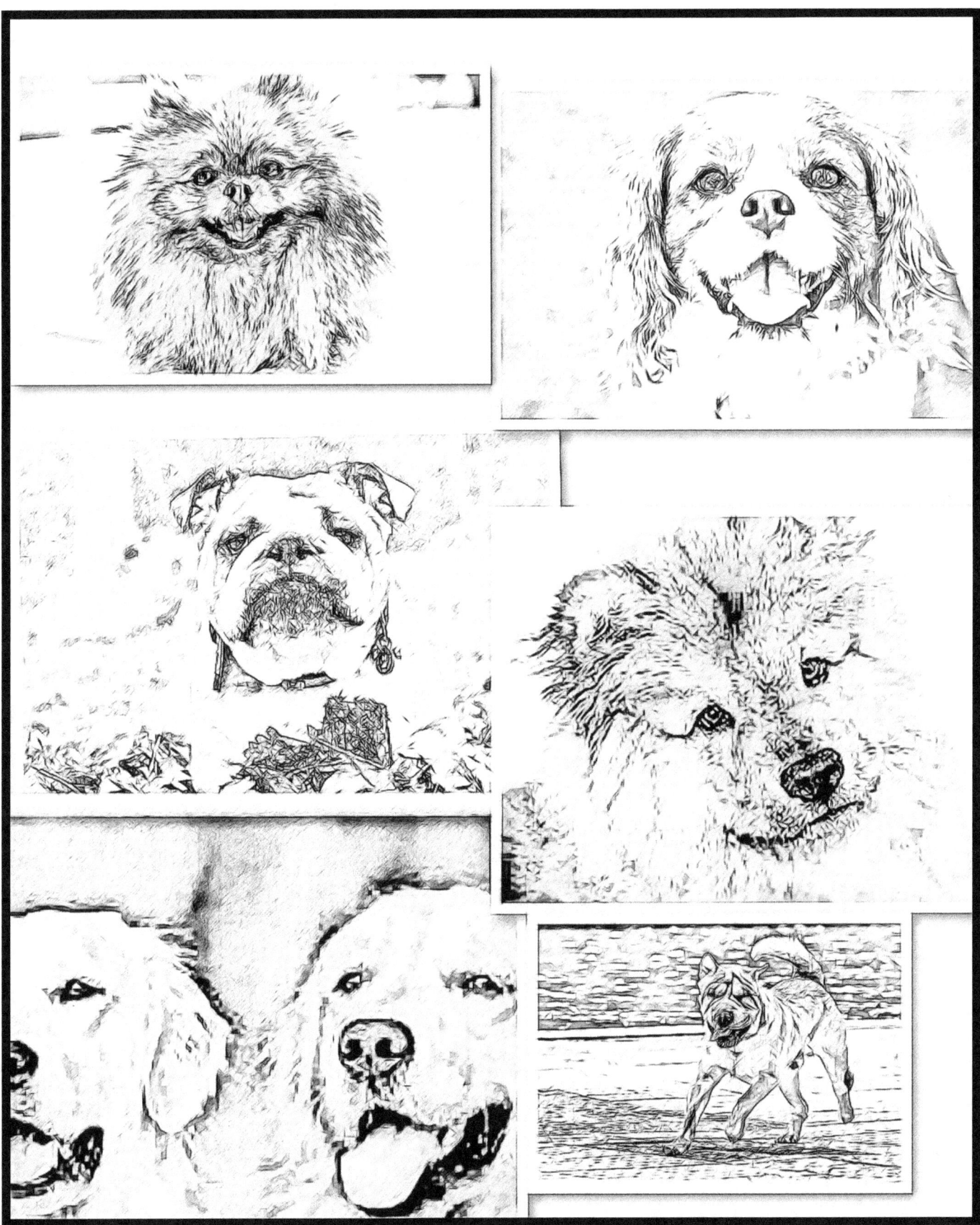

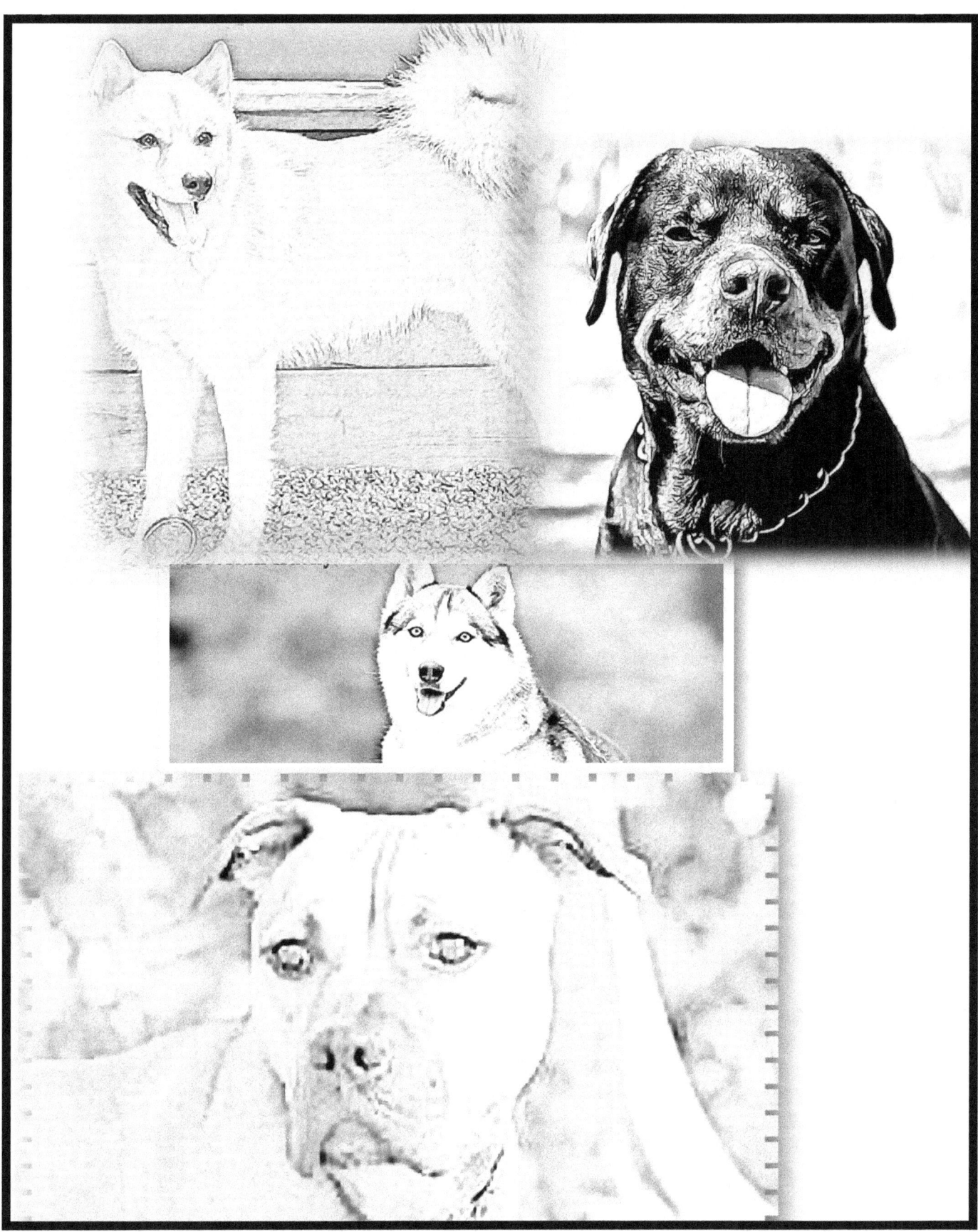

Inspirations, Stress Relieving ... For Stress Relieving and Relaxing

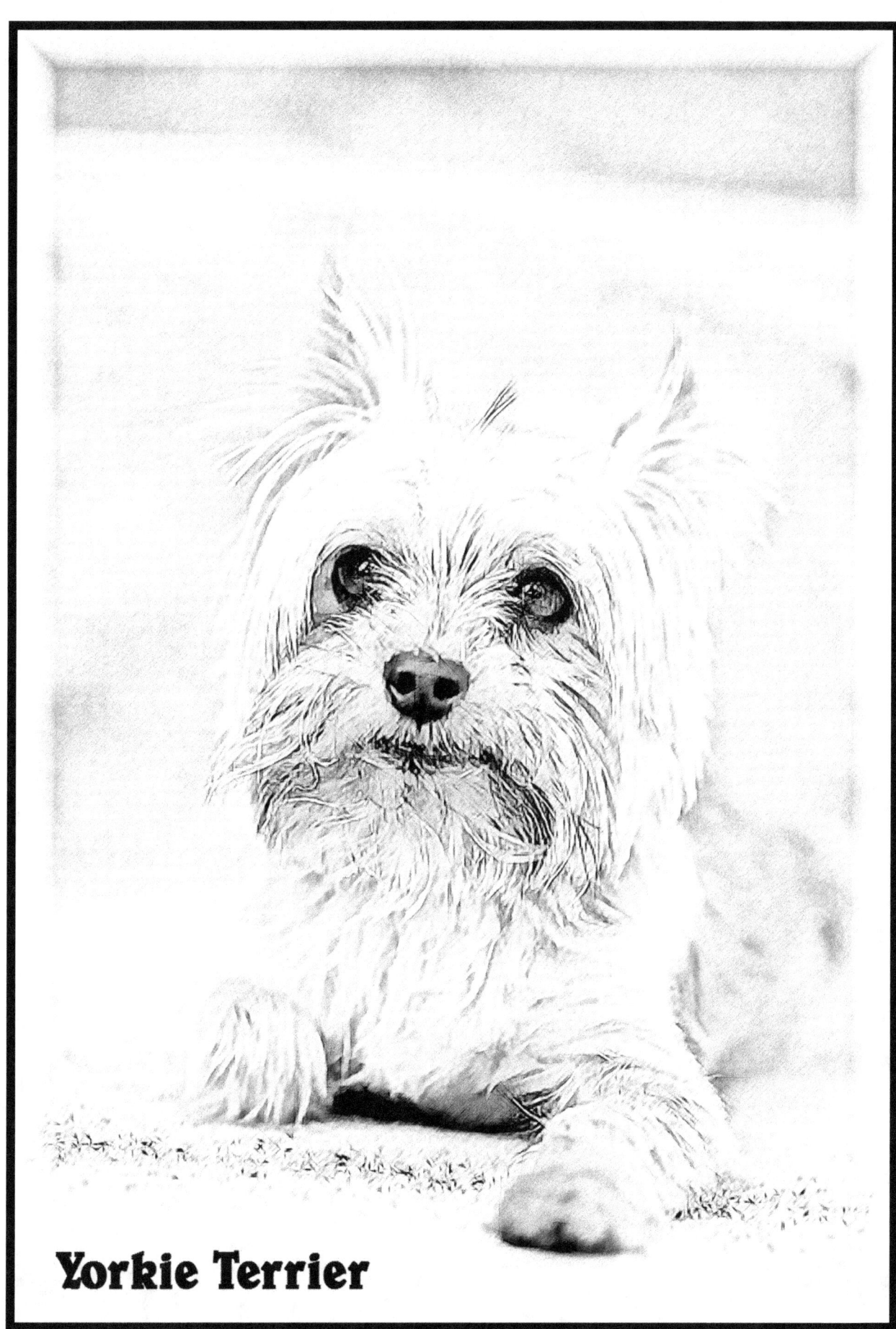

Yorkie Terrier

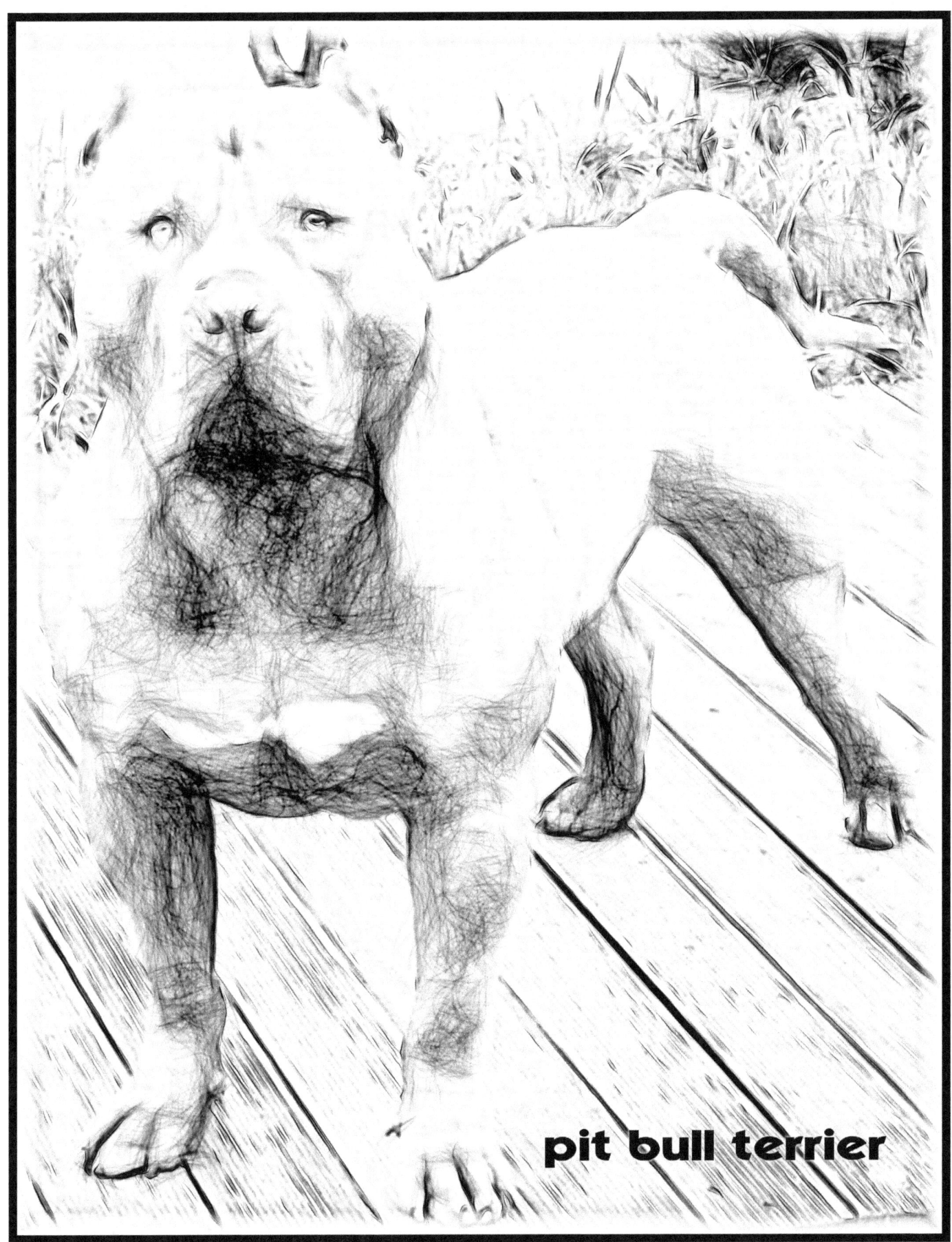

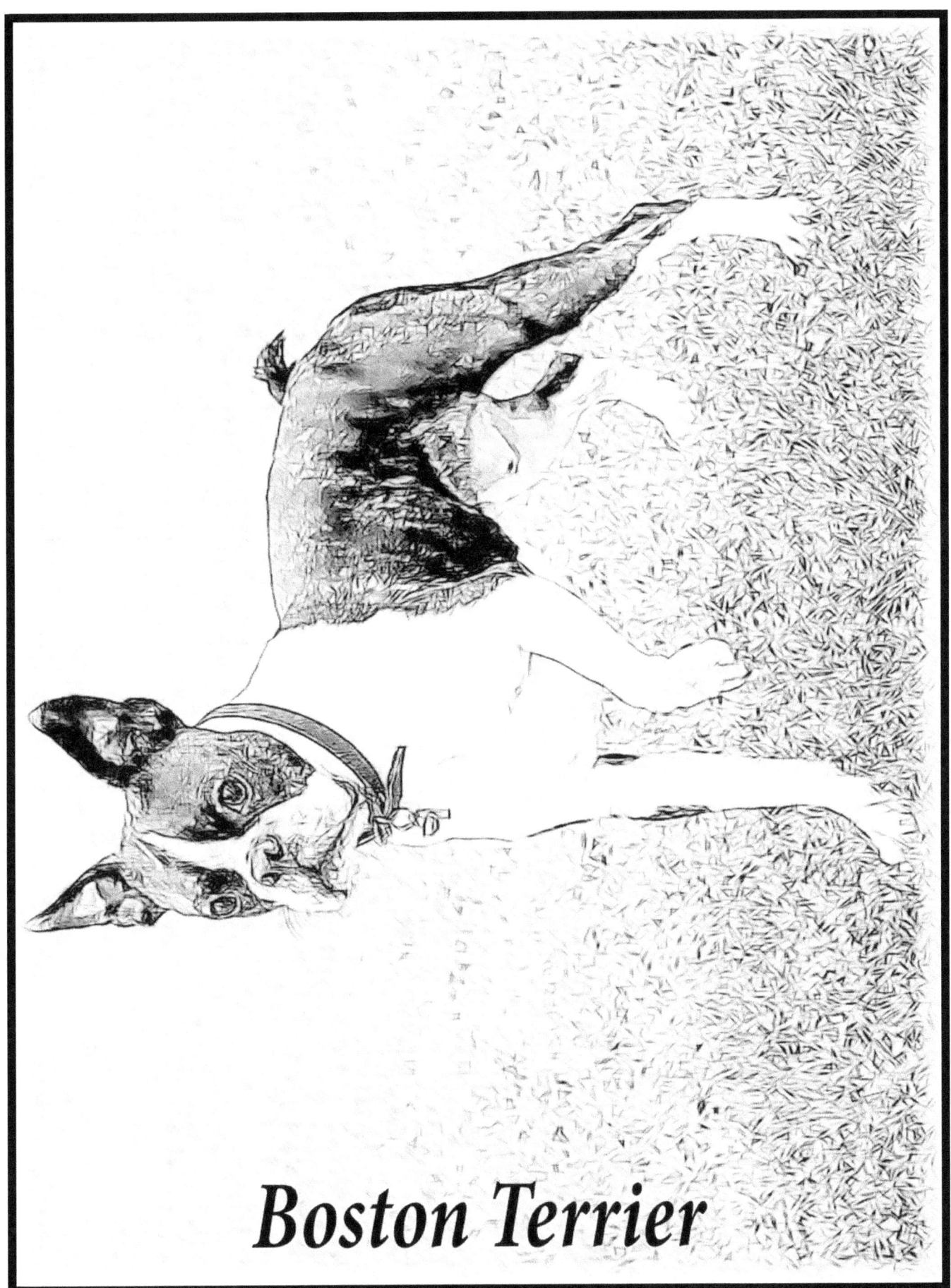
Boston Terrier

AUSTRALIAN CATTLE DOG

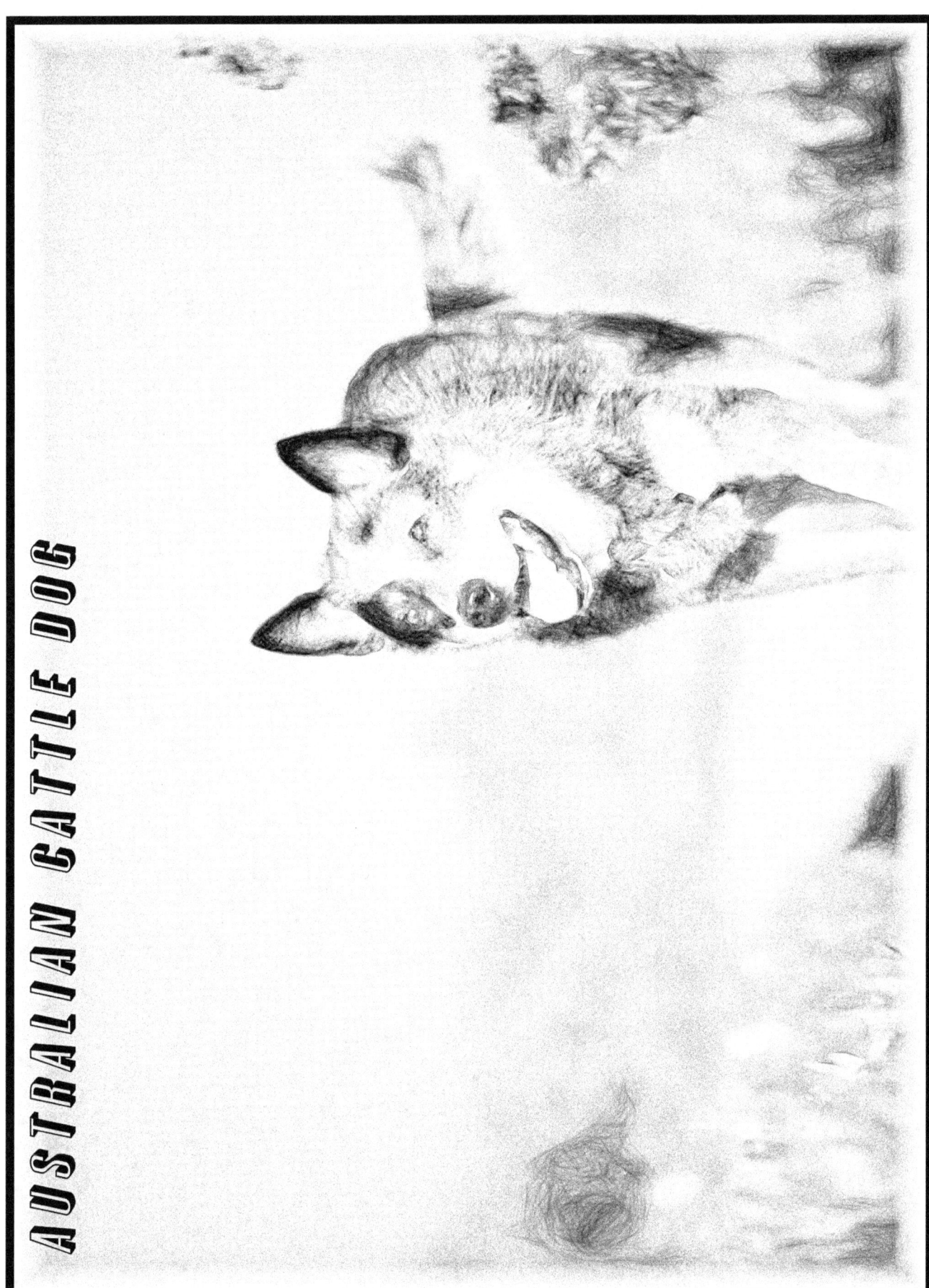

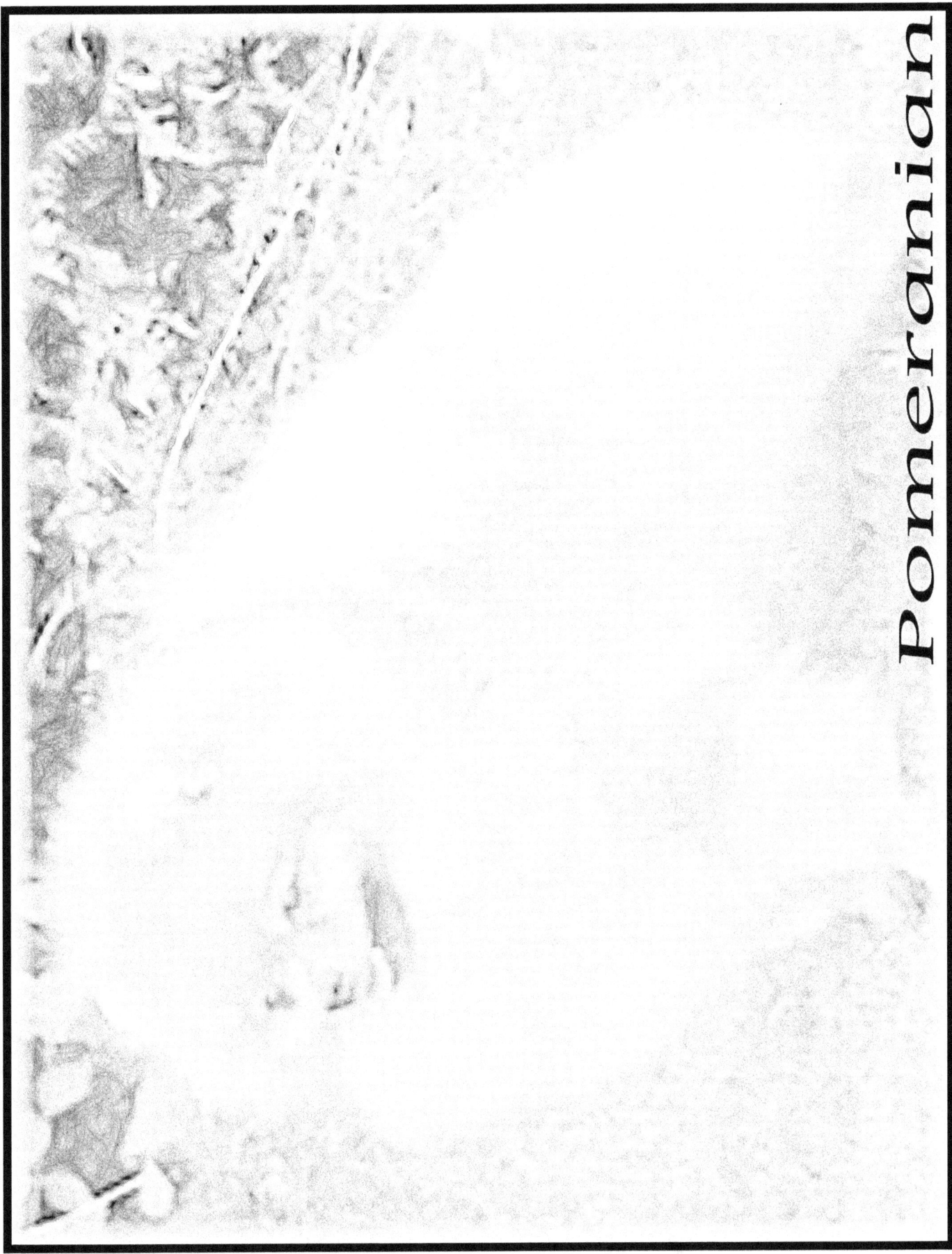

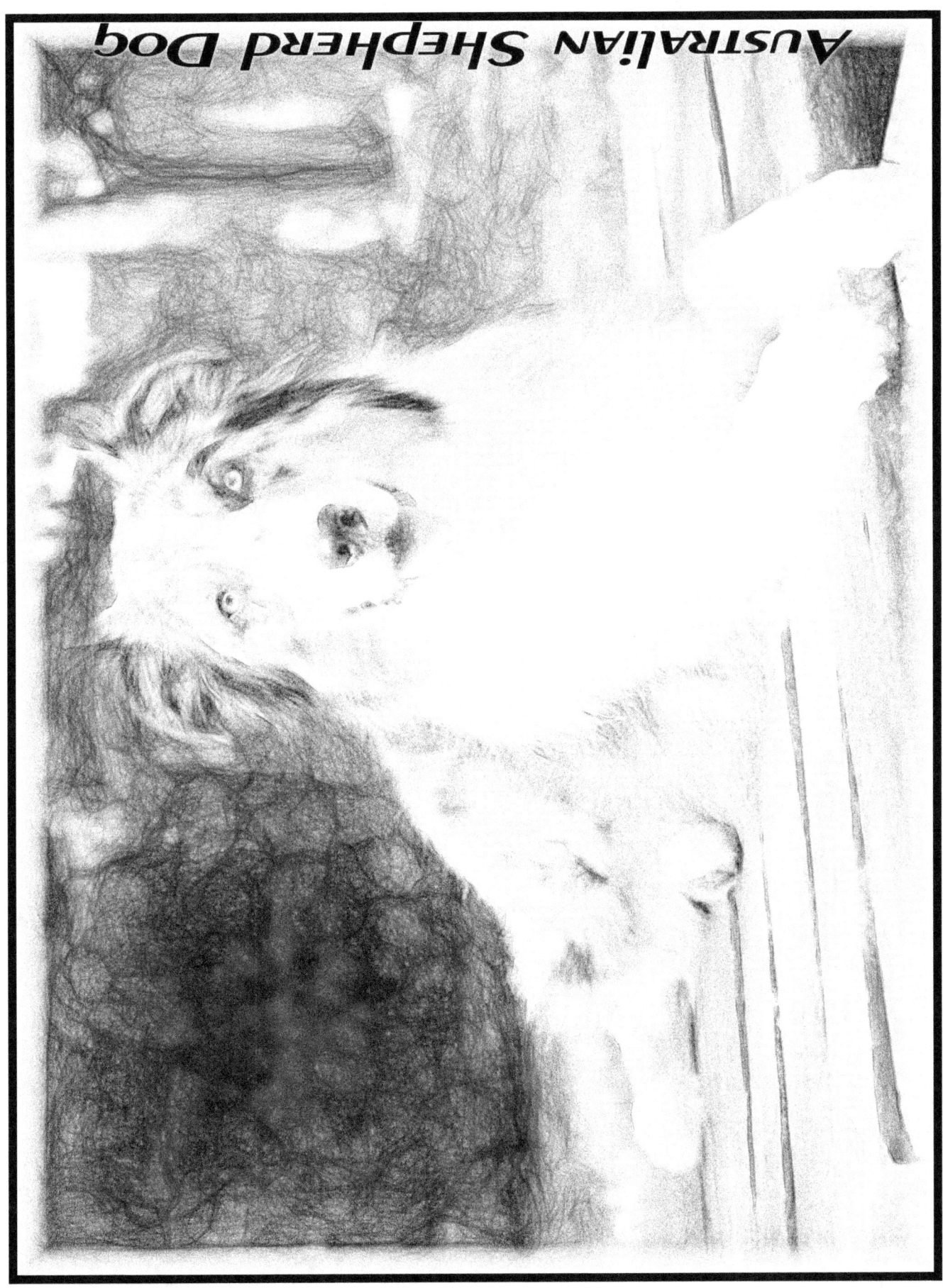
Australian Shepherd Dog

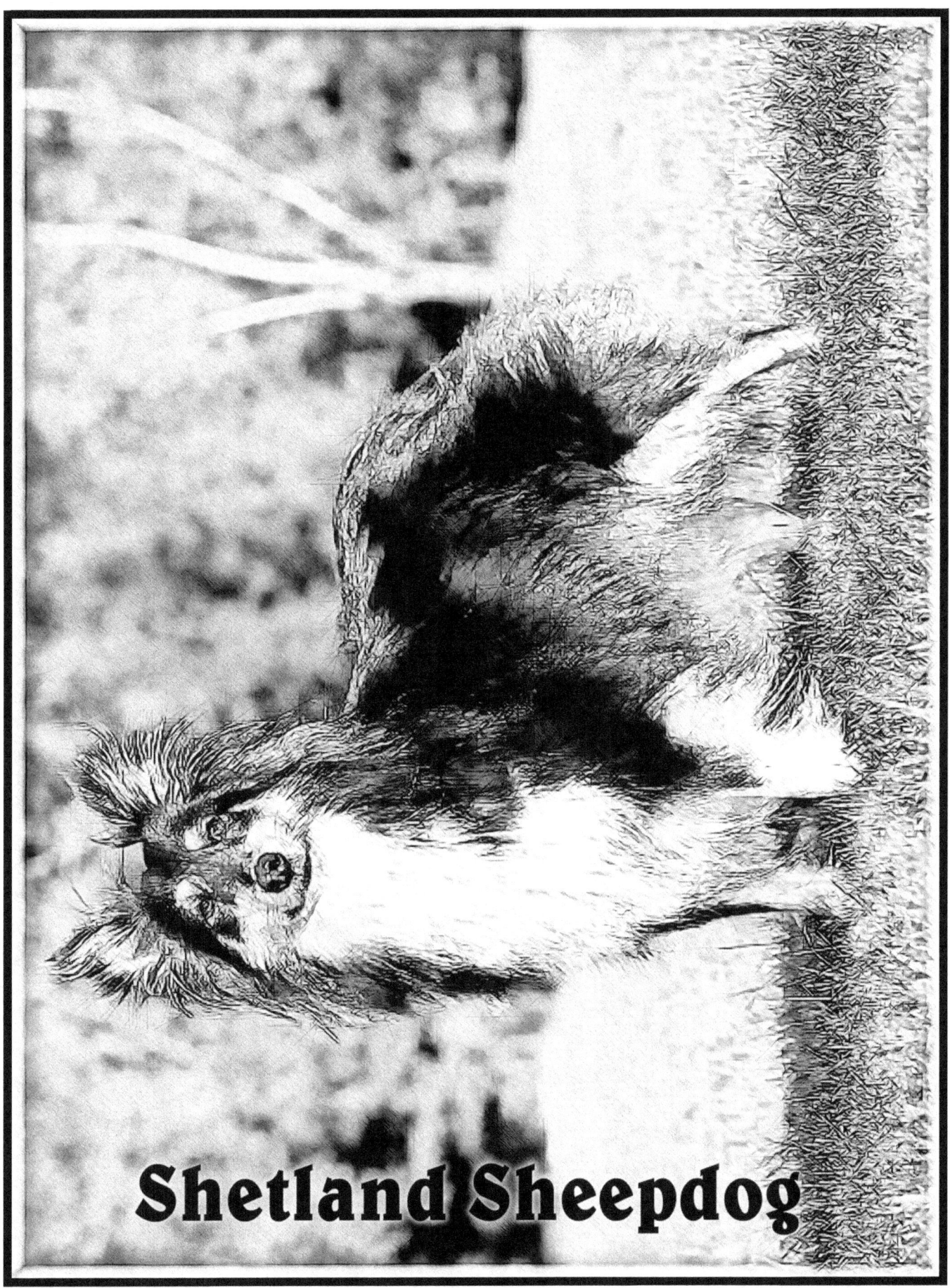

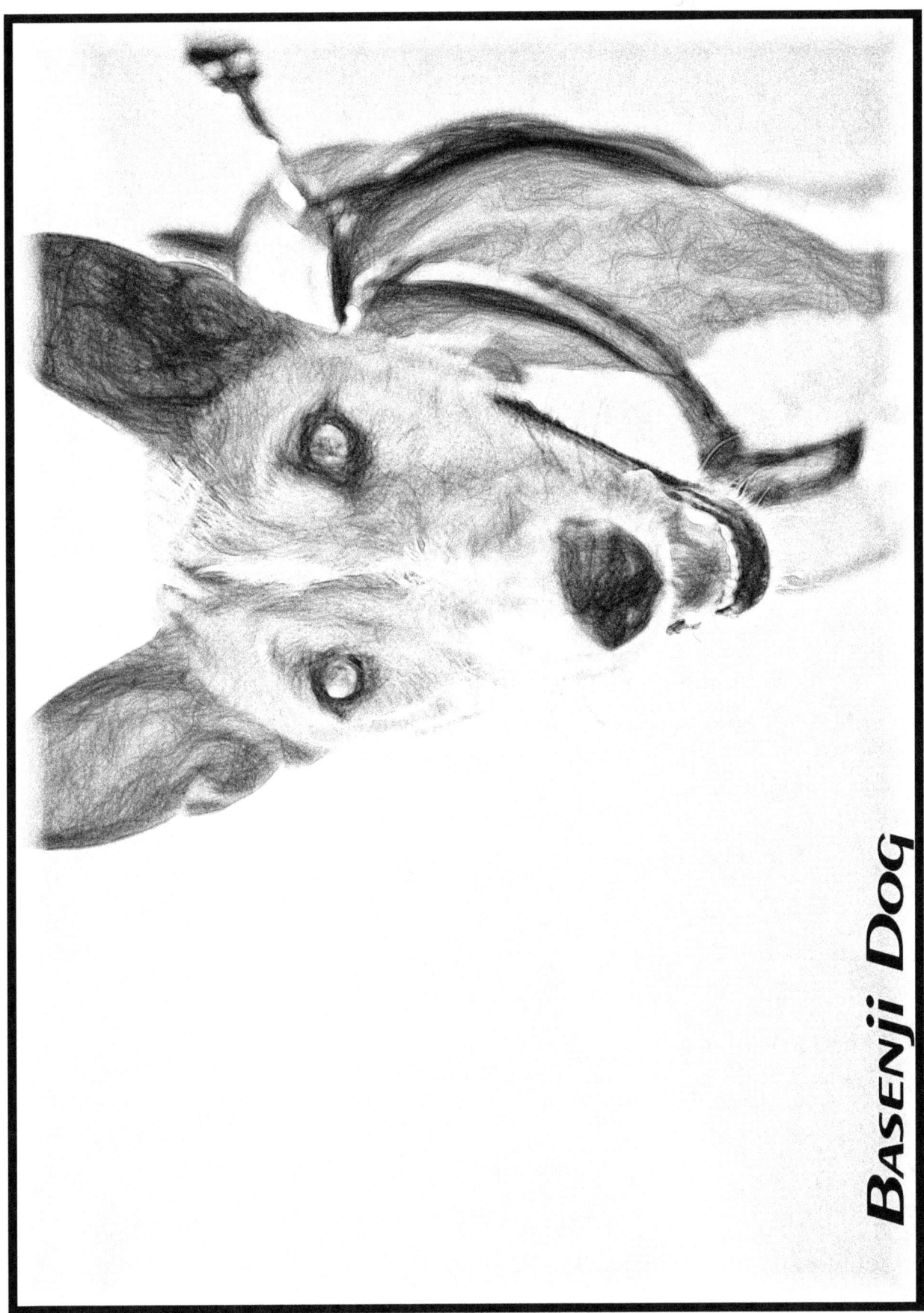
Basenji Dog

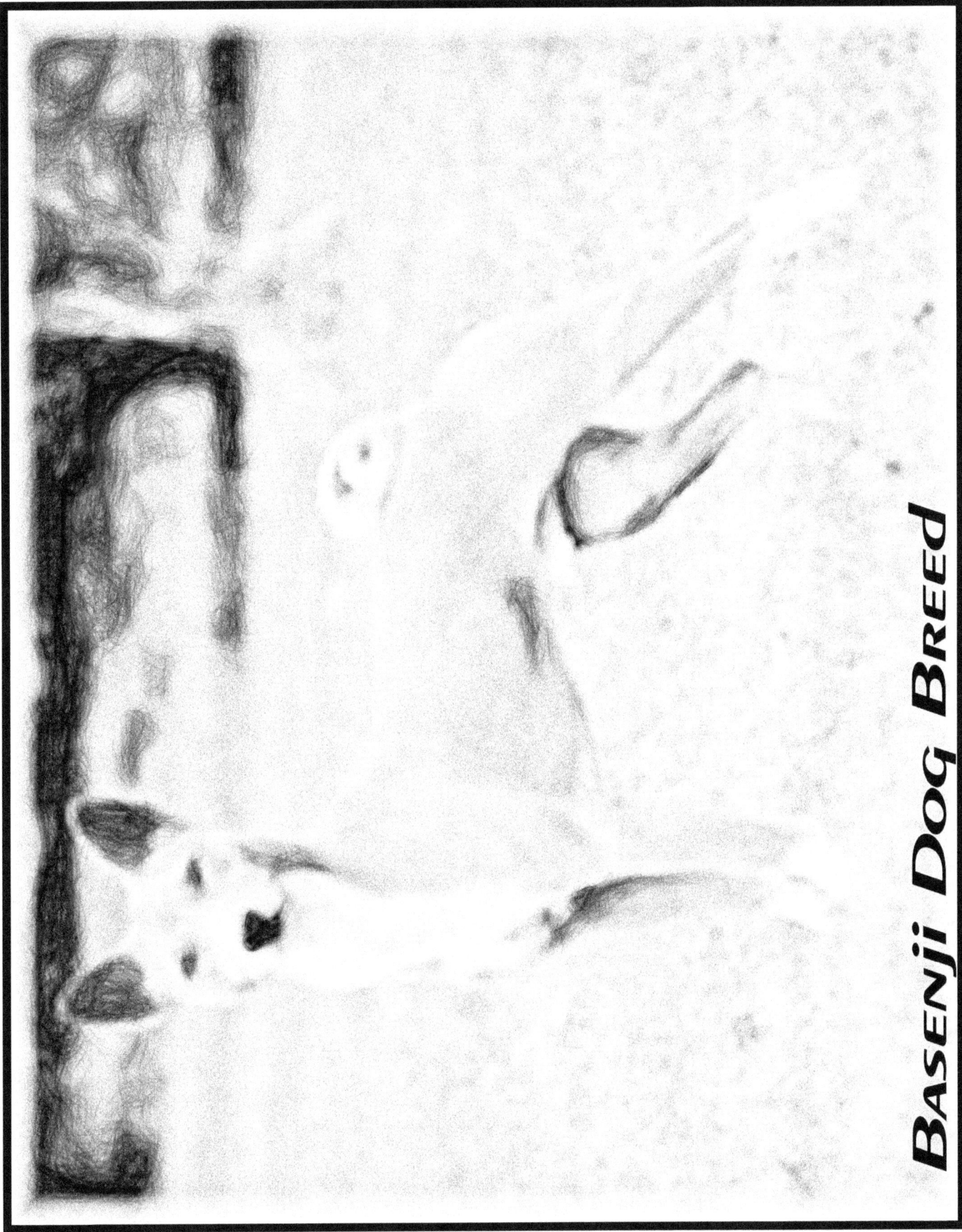

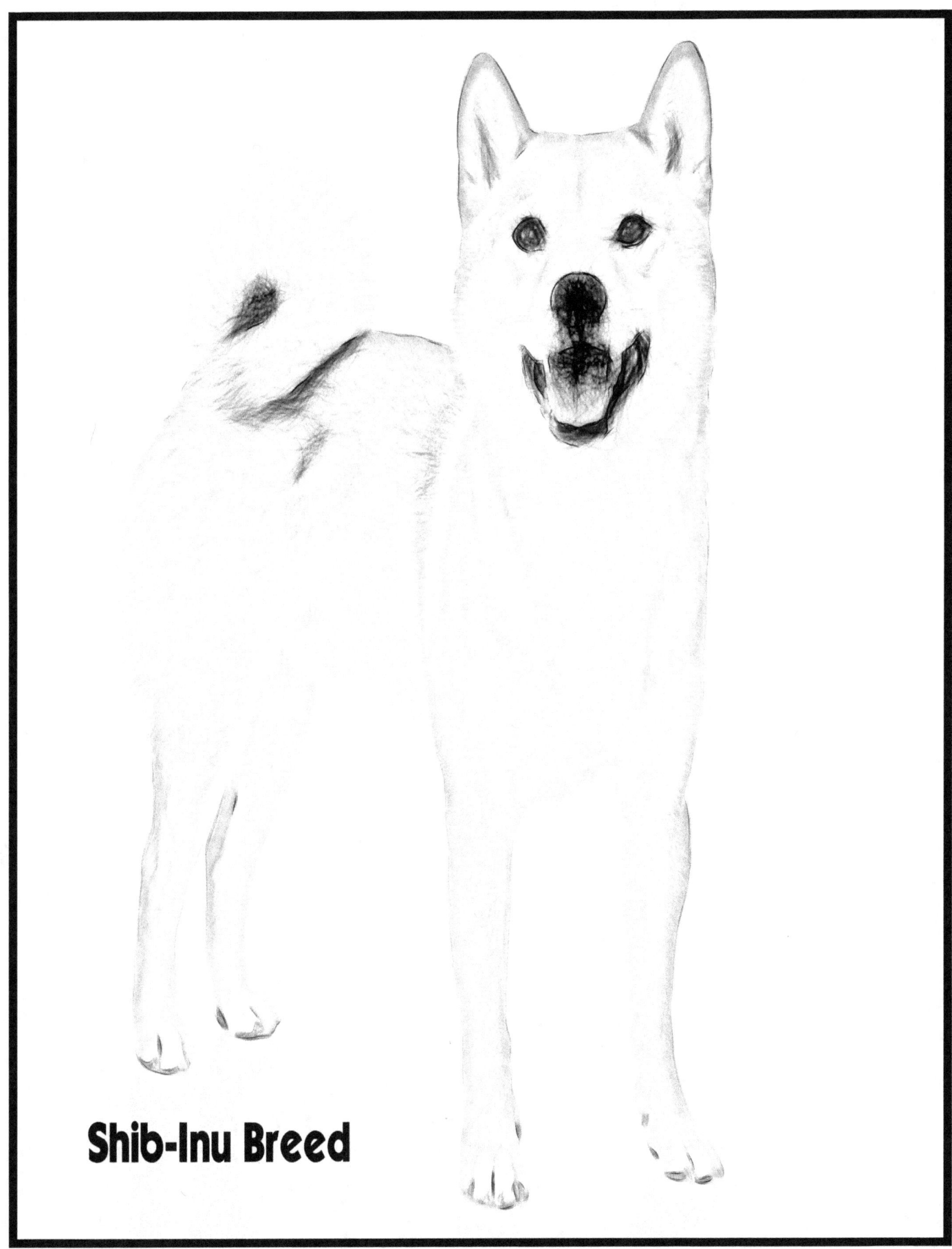

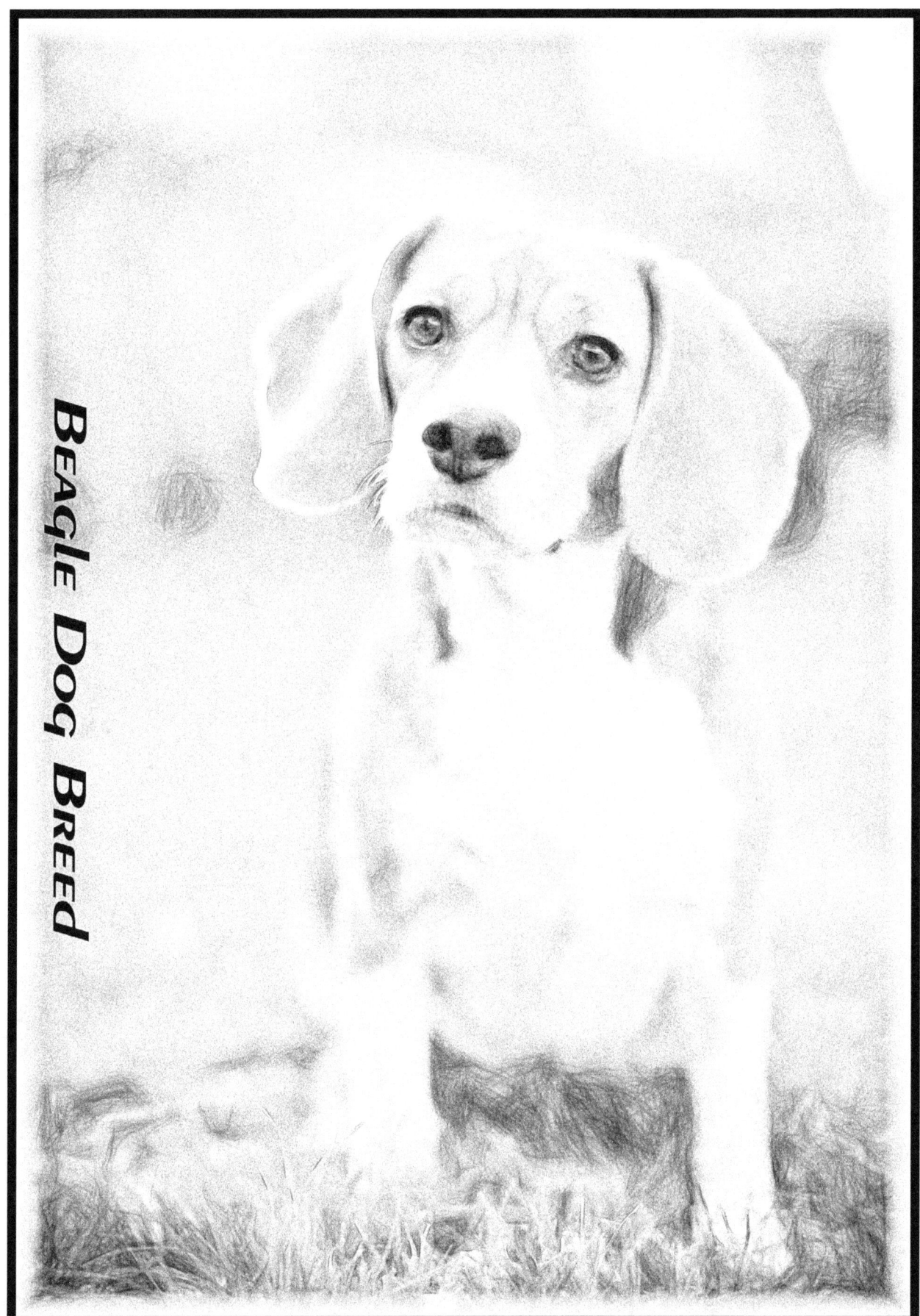

Beagle Dog Breed

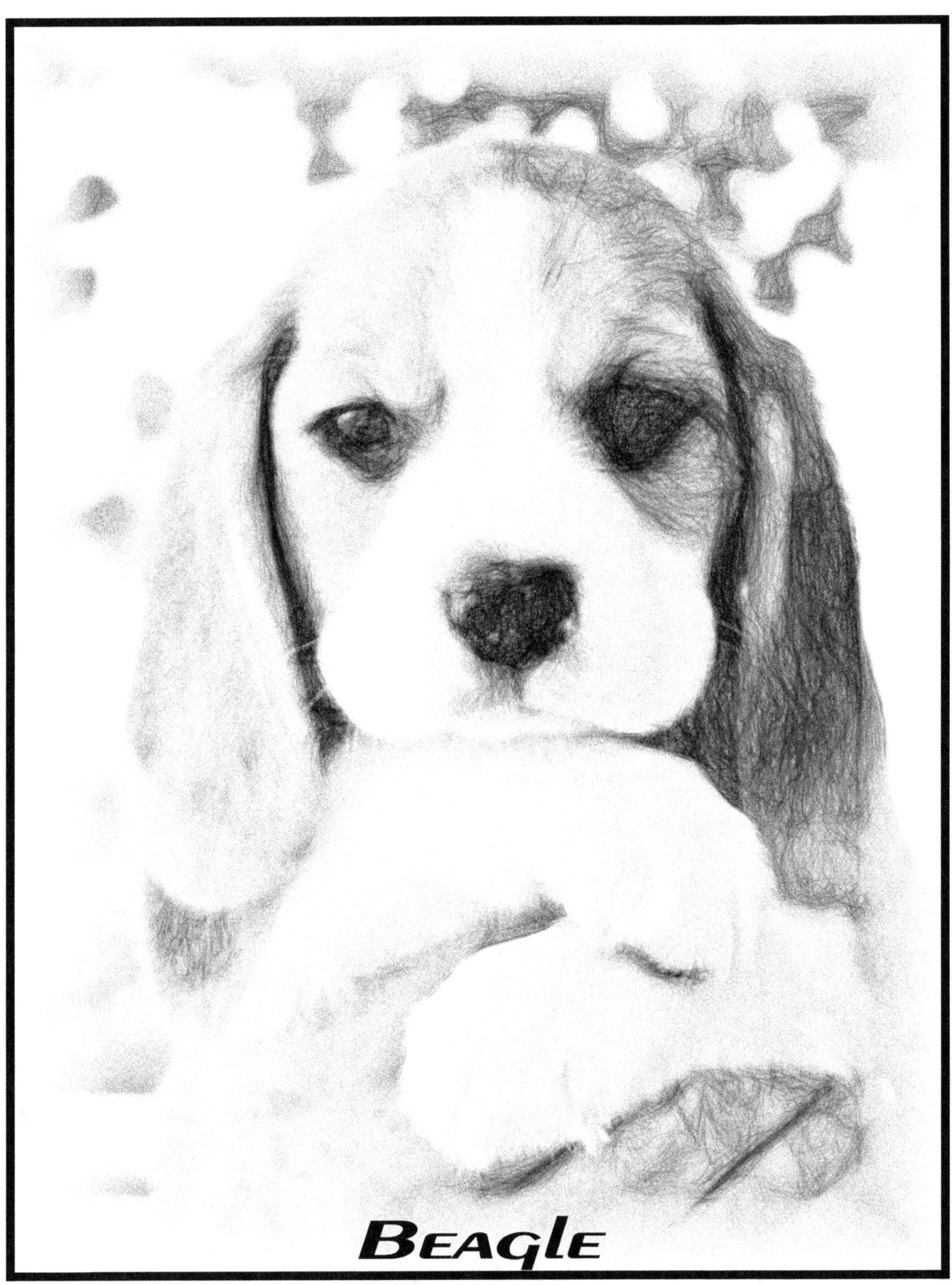

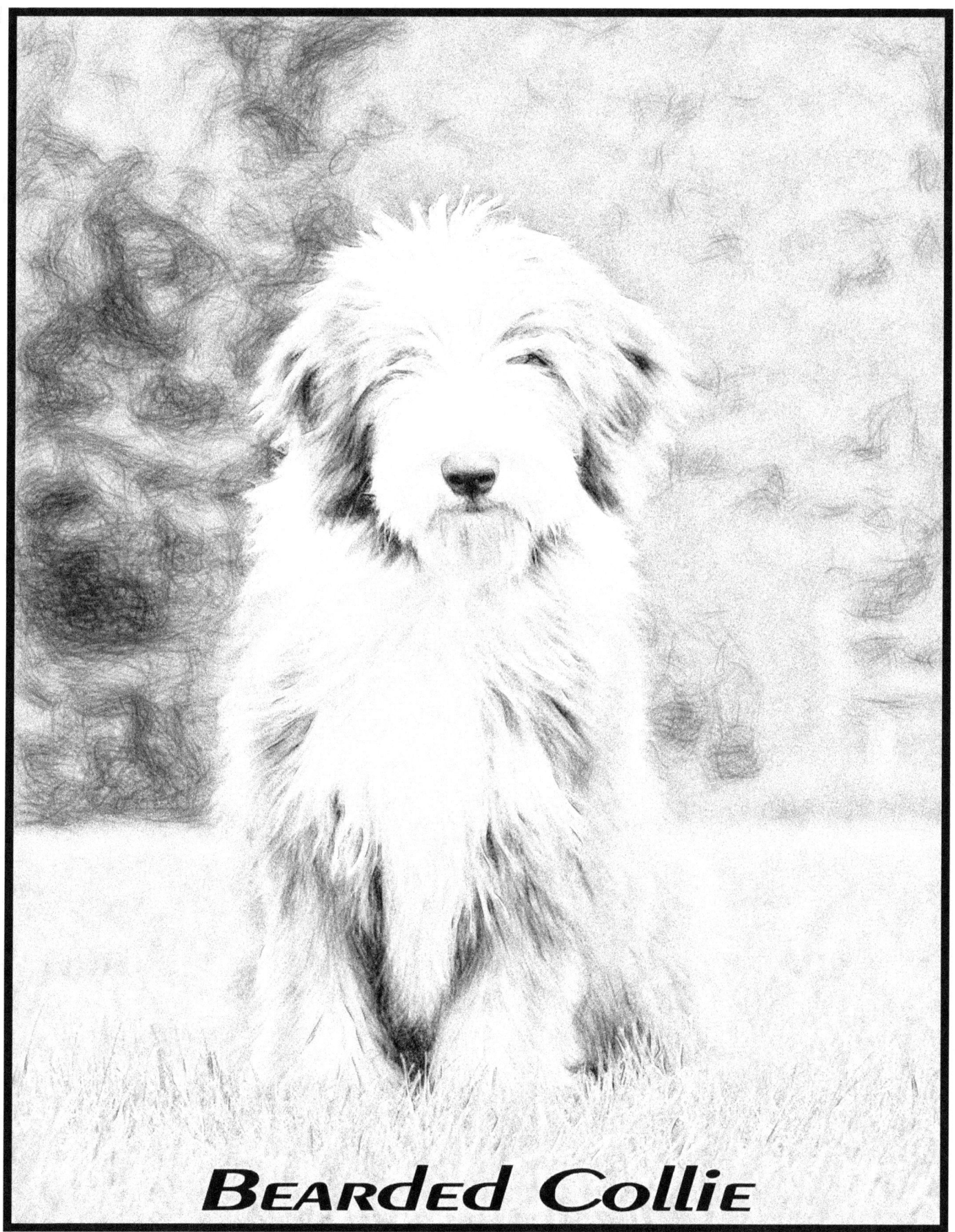

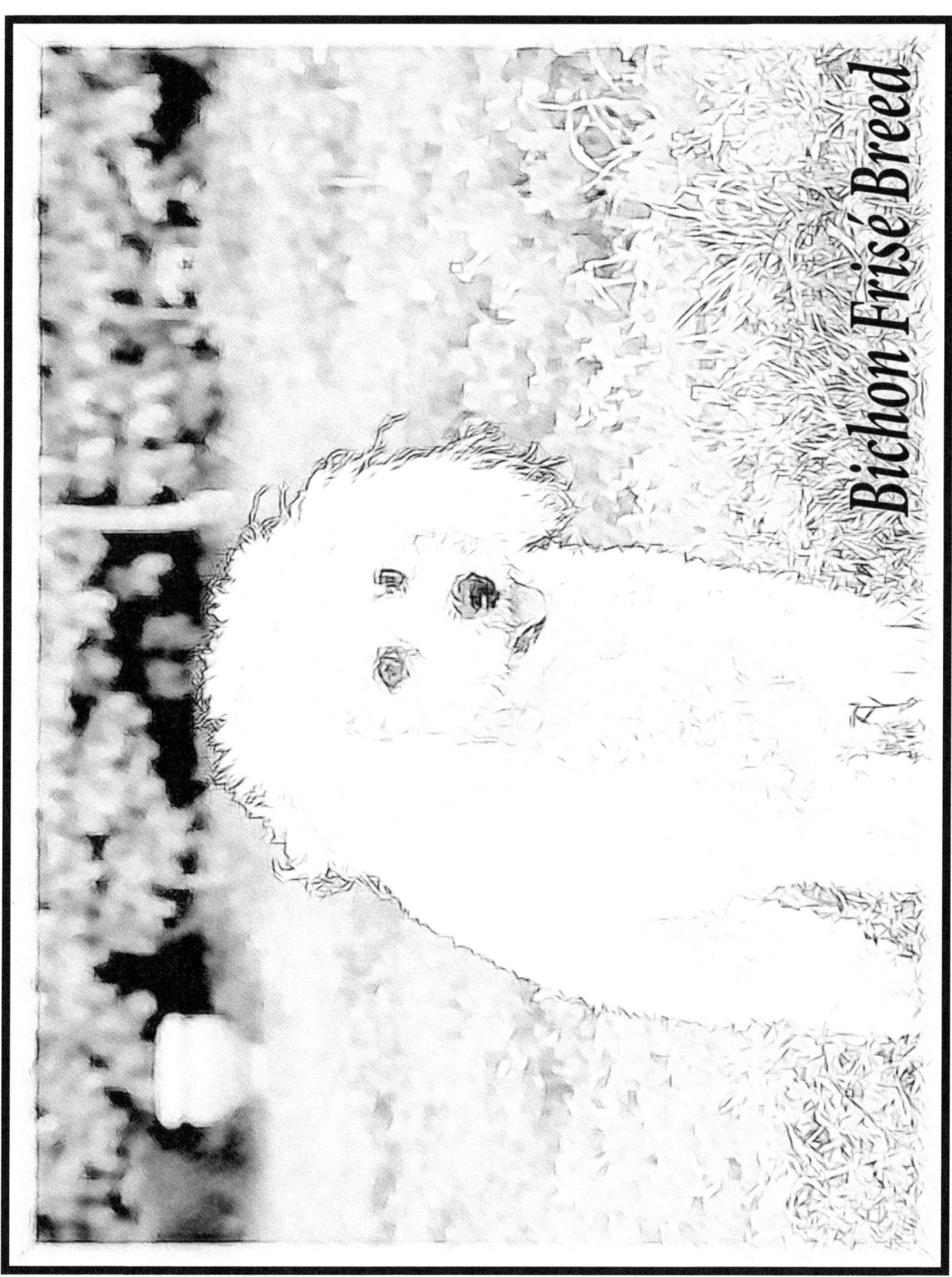

Bichon Frise Breed

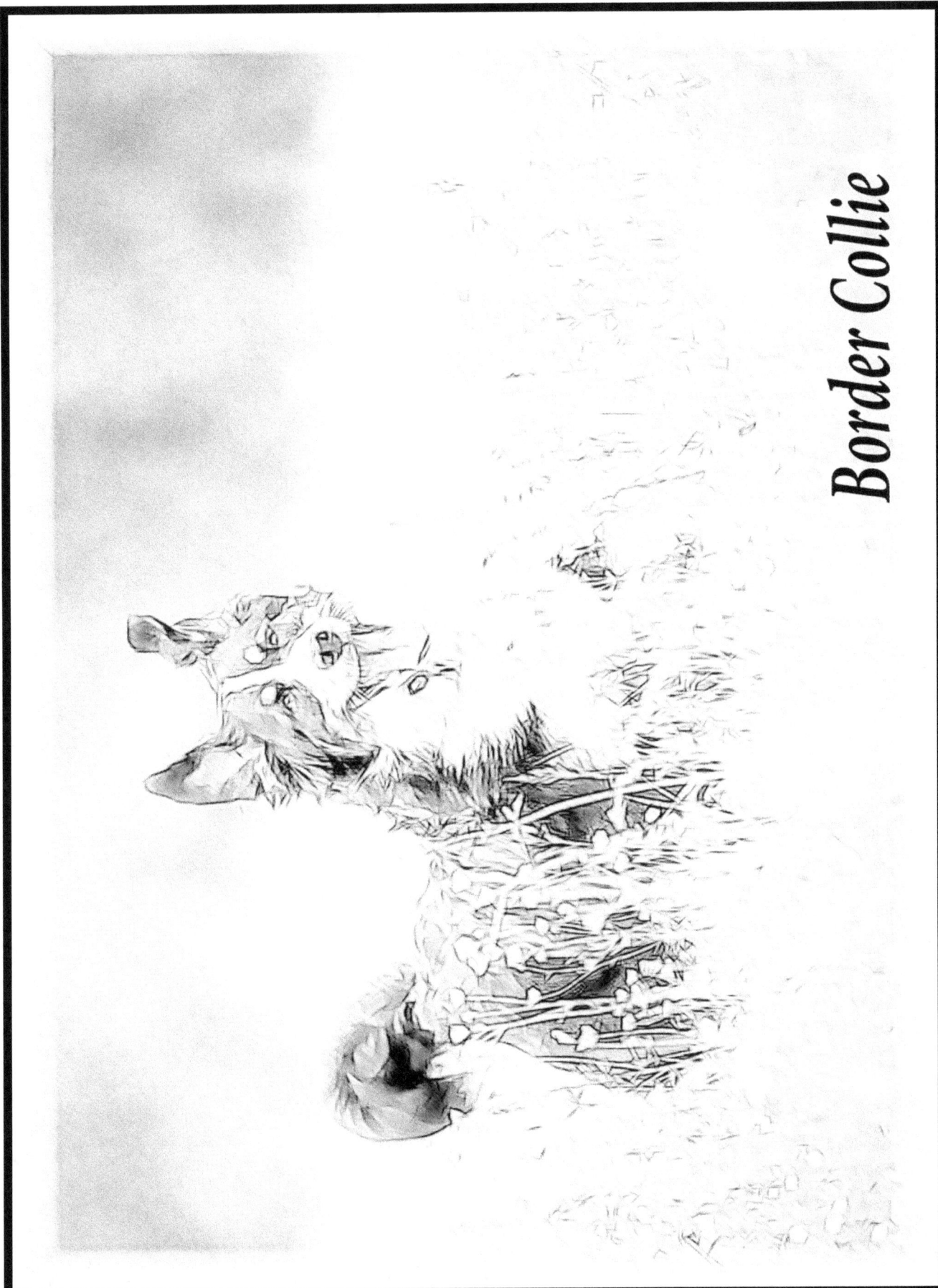

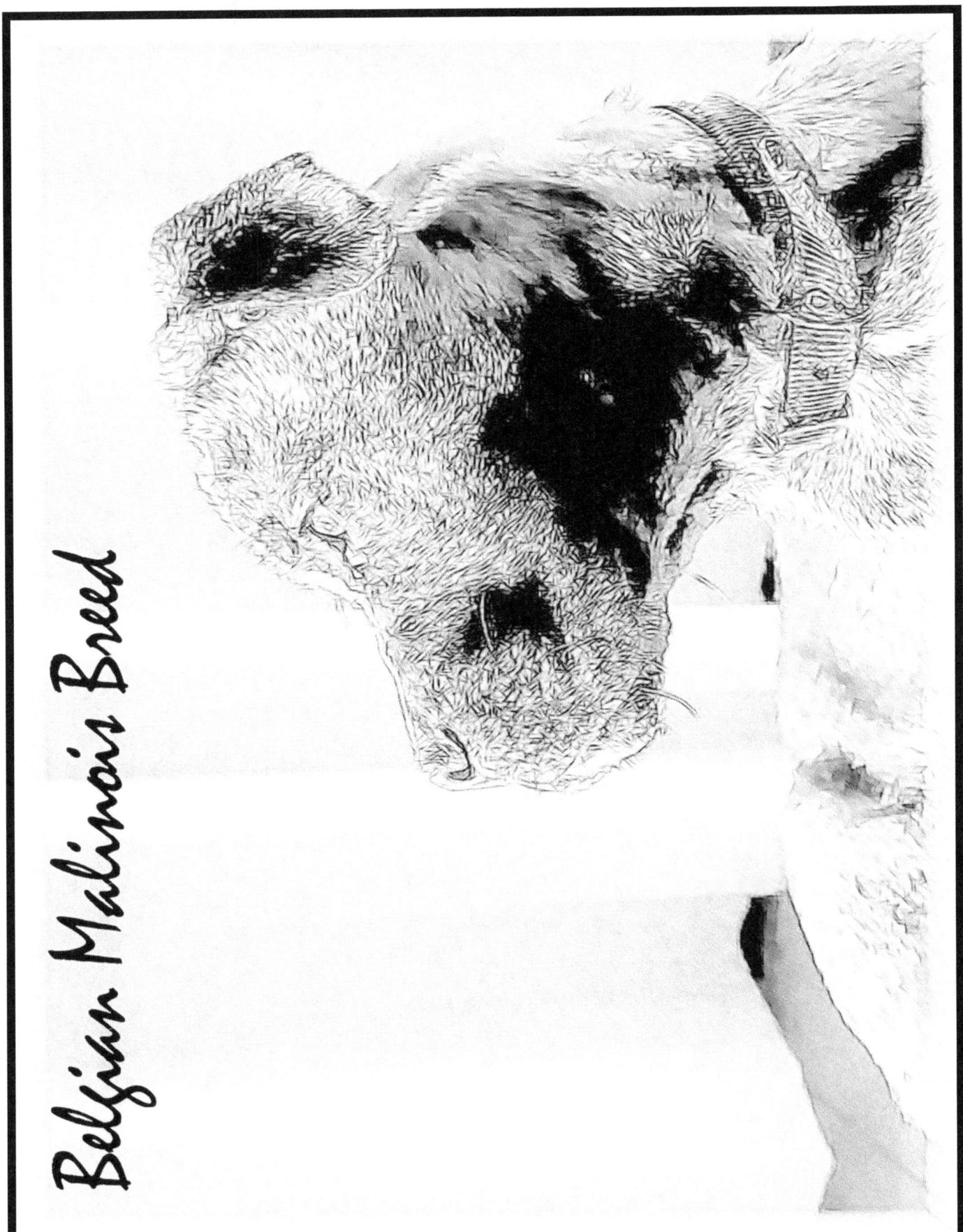

Belgian Malinois Breed

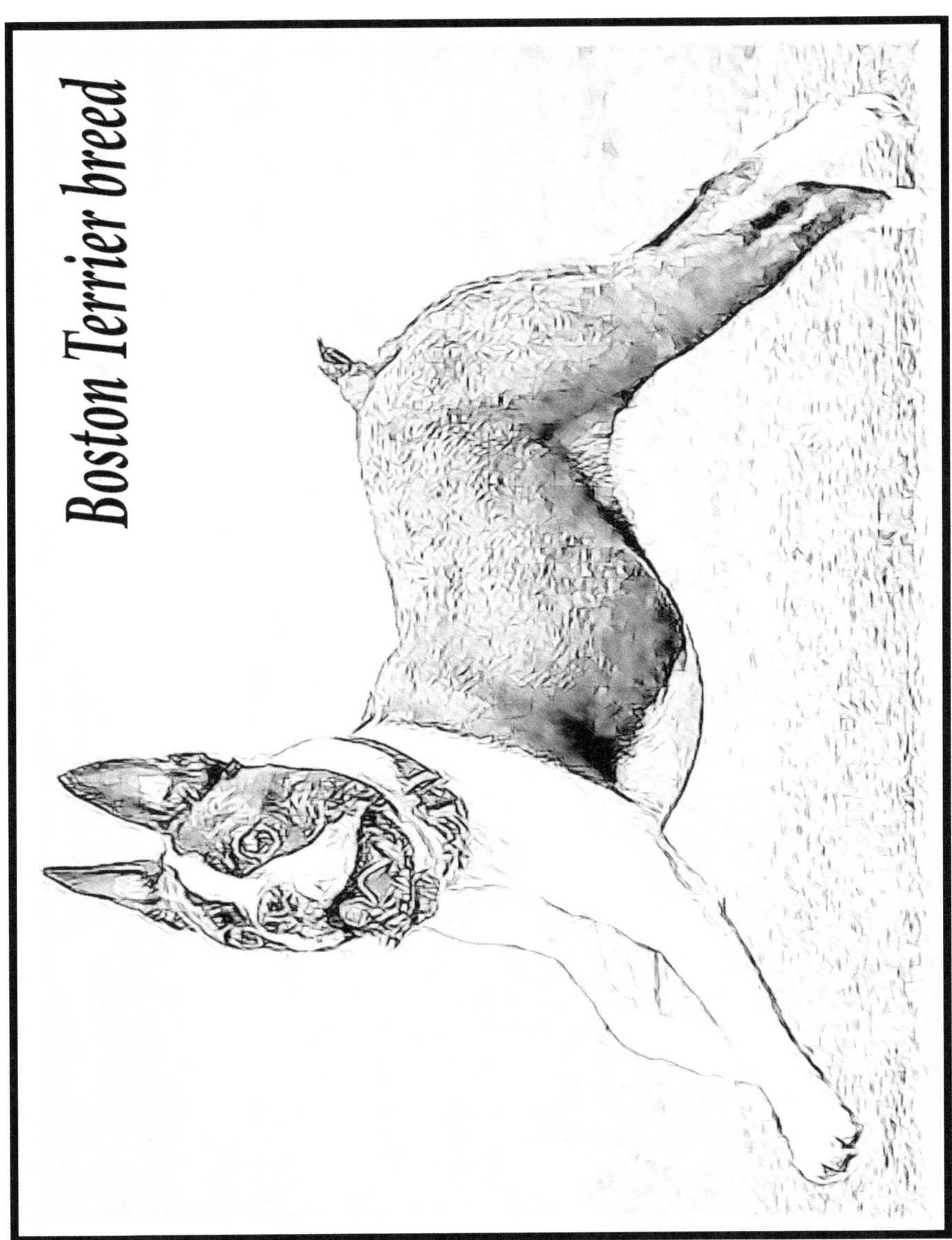

Boston Terrier Terrier breed

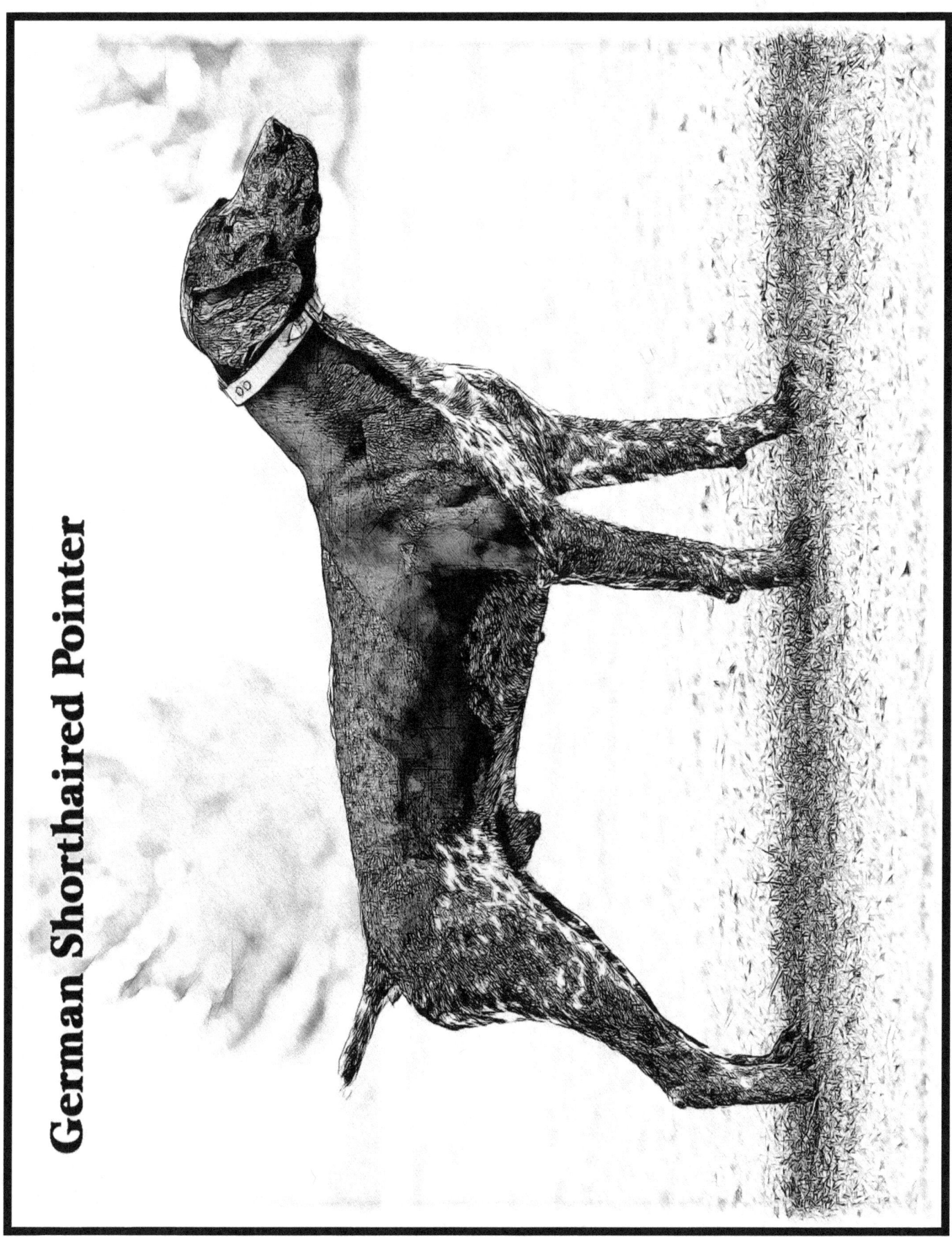

Great Dane Wimaraner

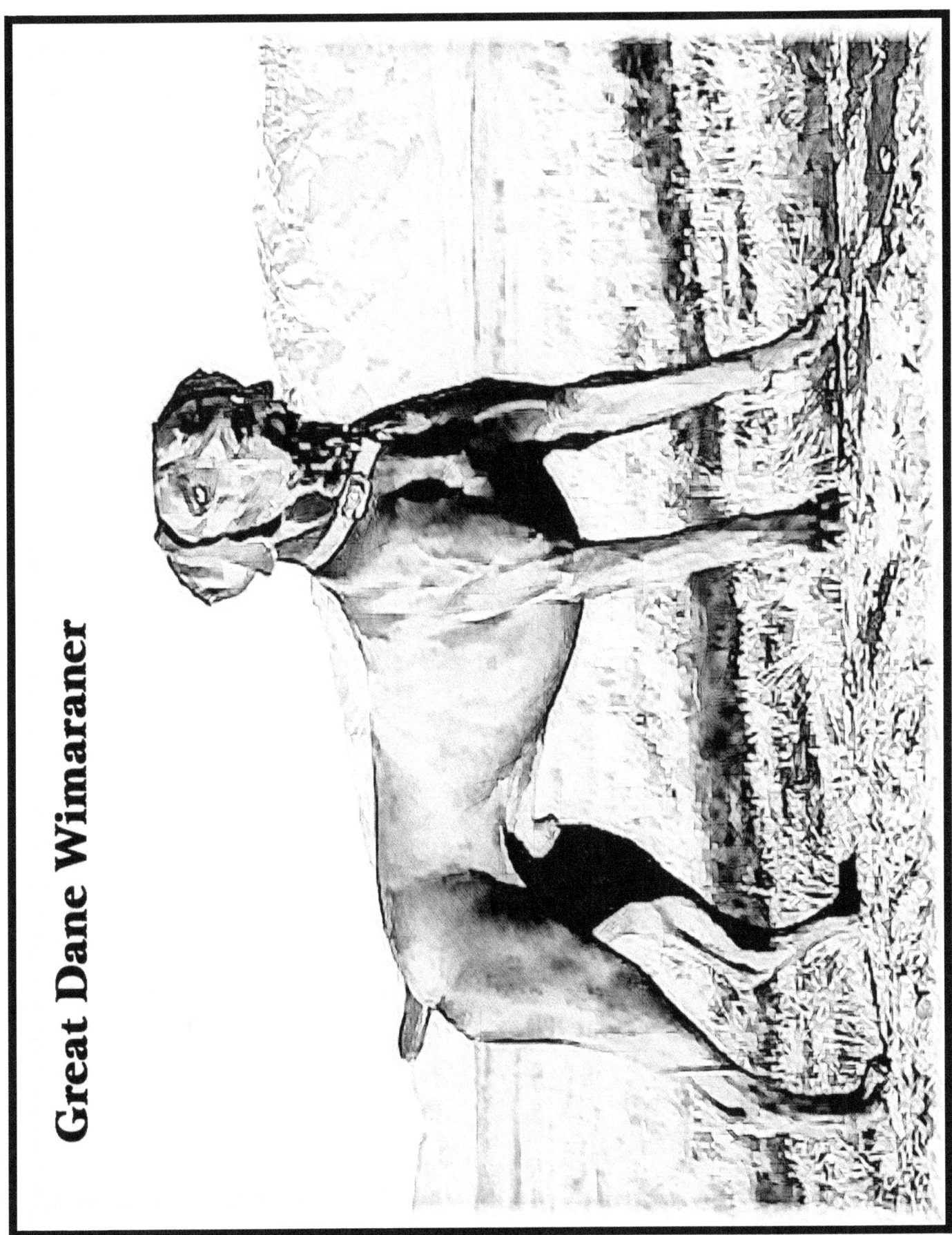

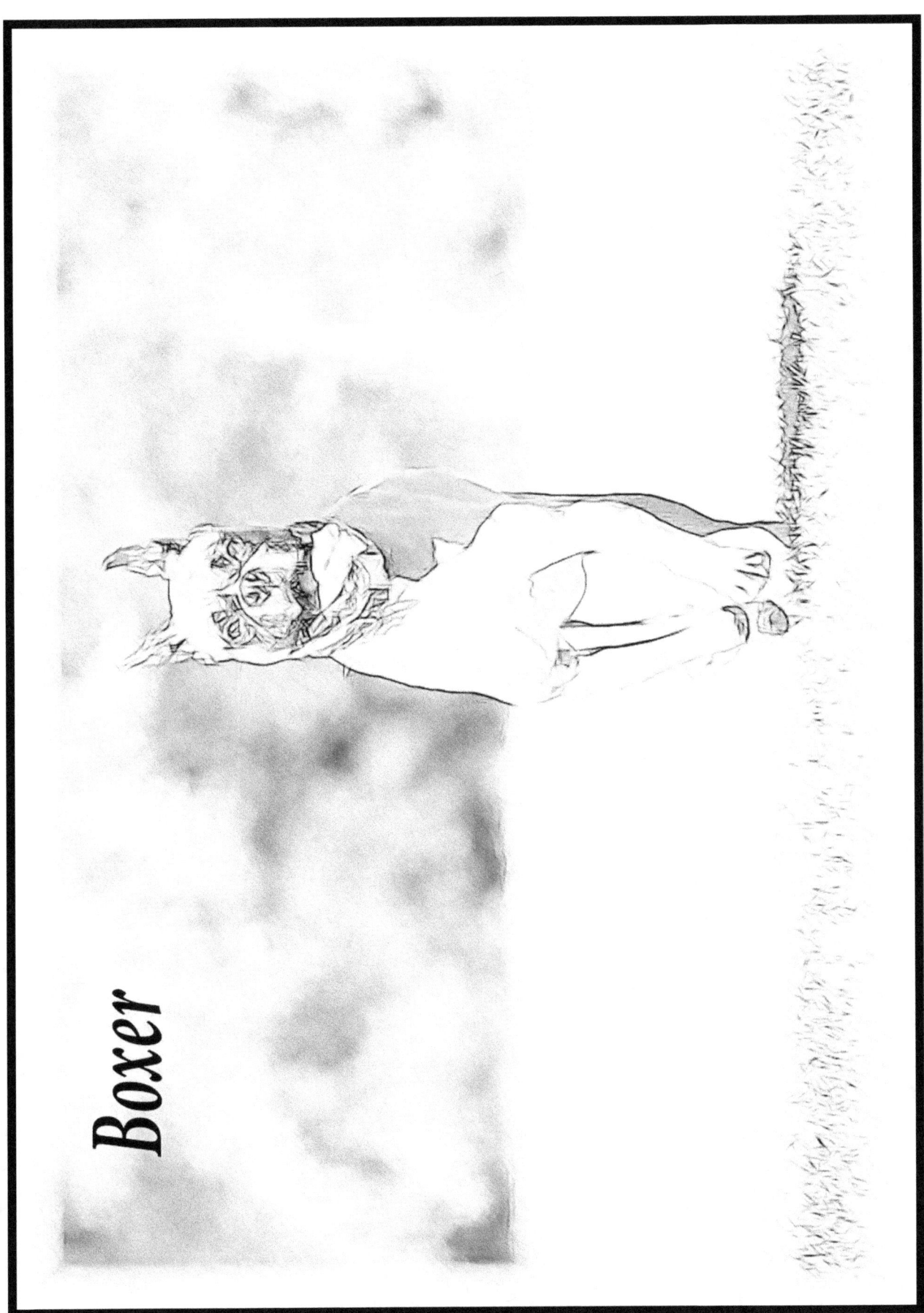
Boxer

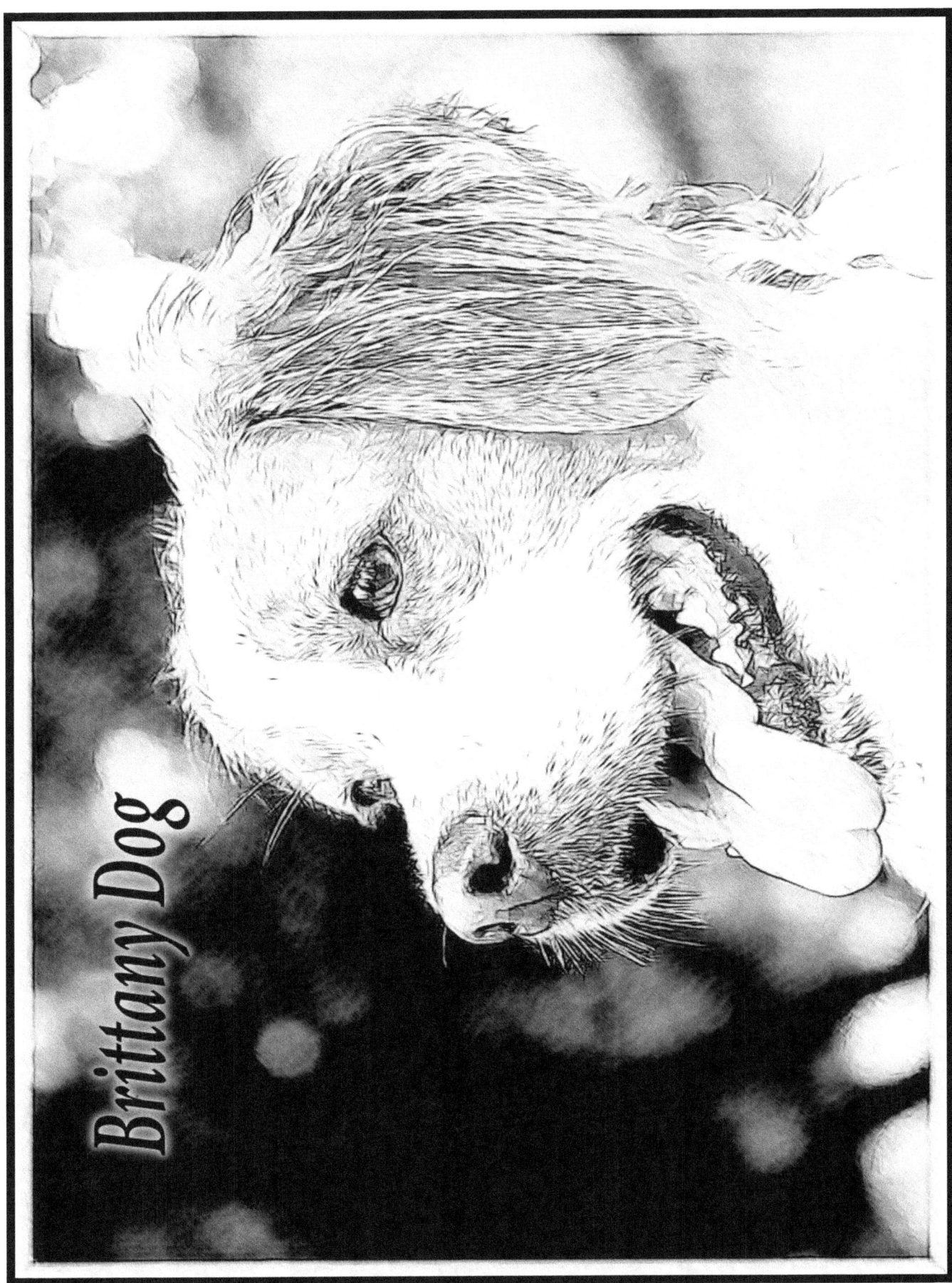

Bull Terrier

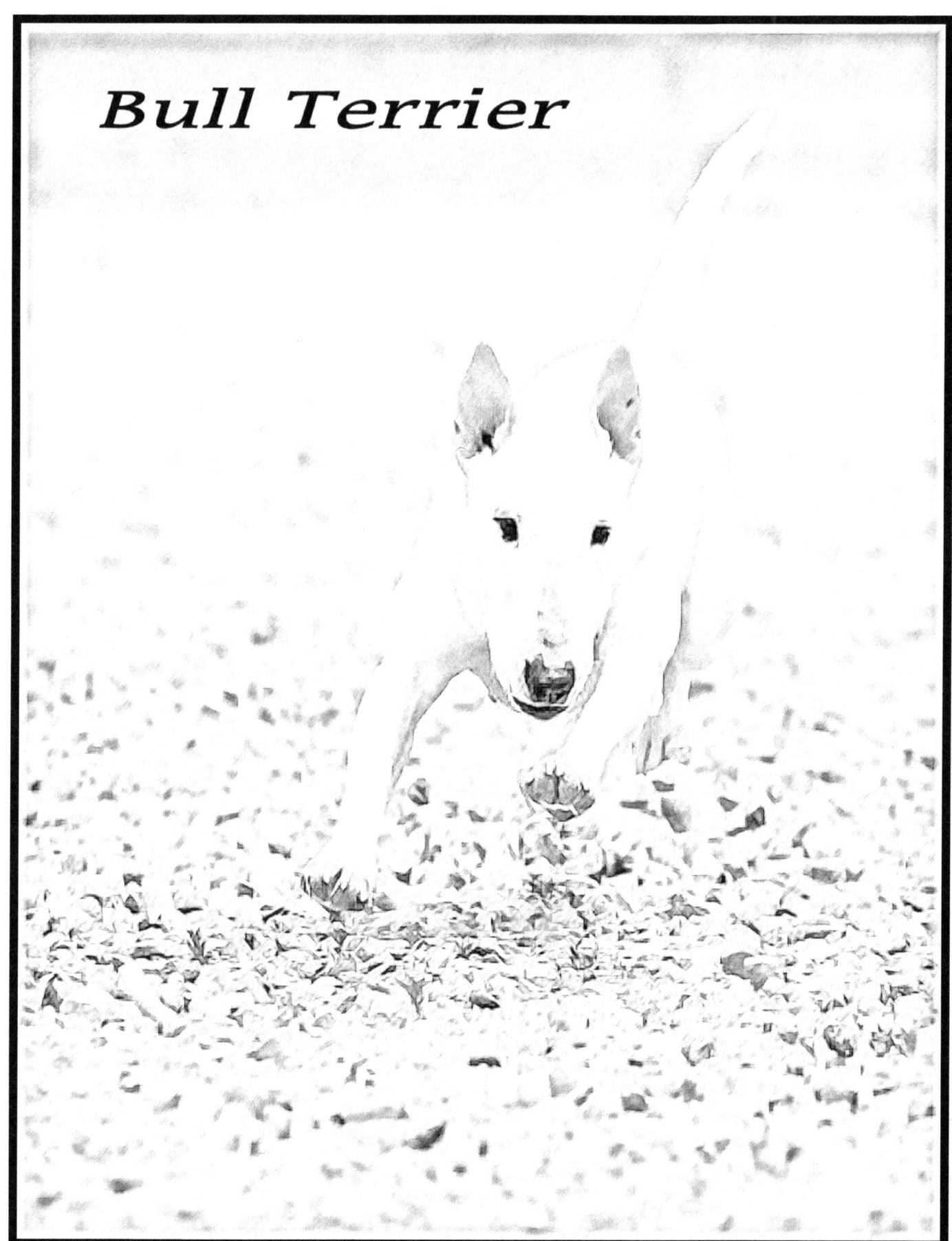

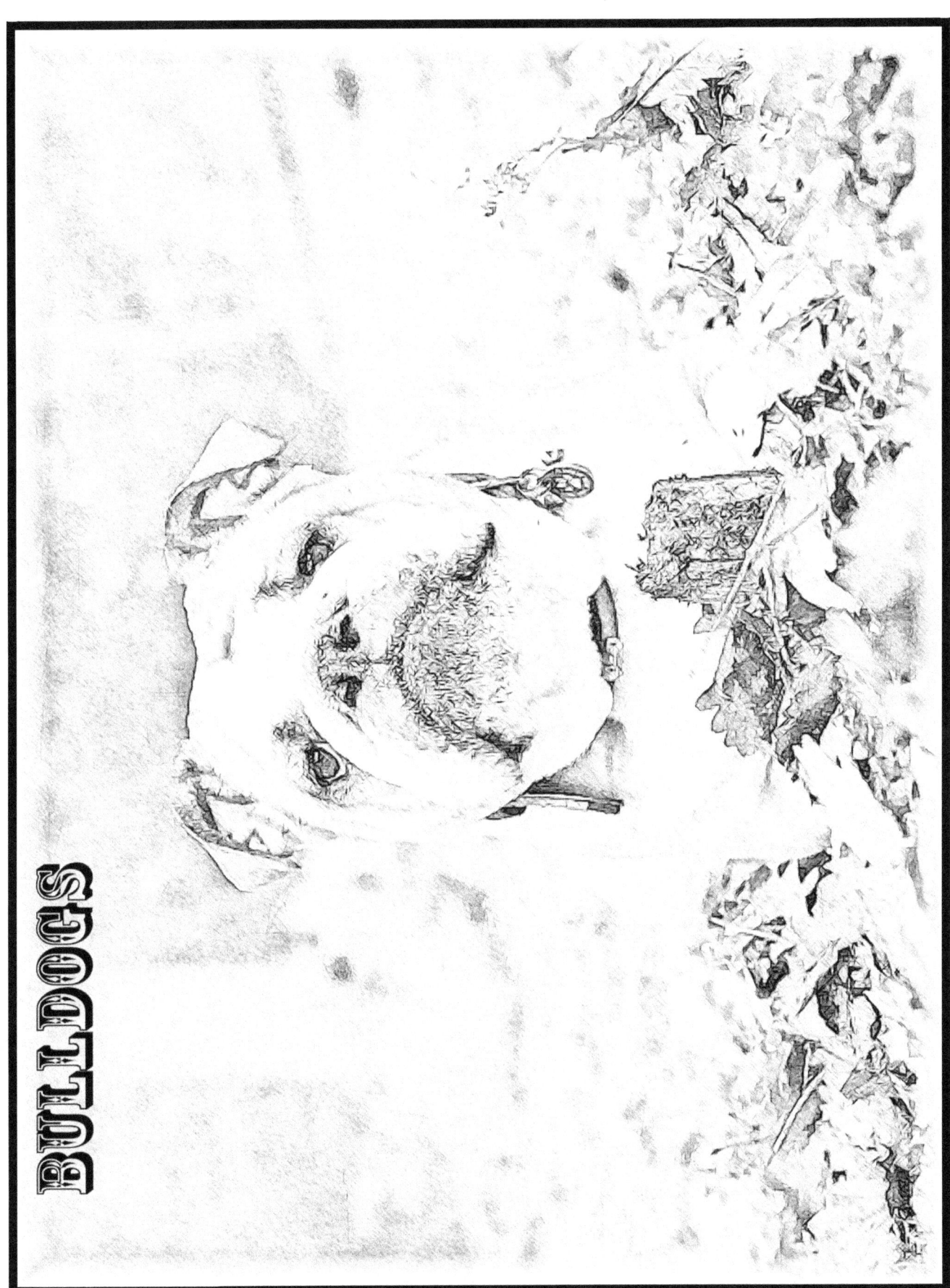

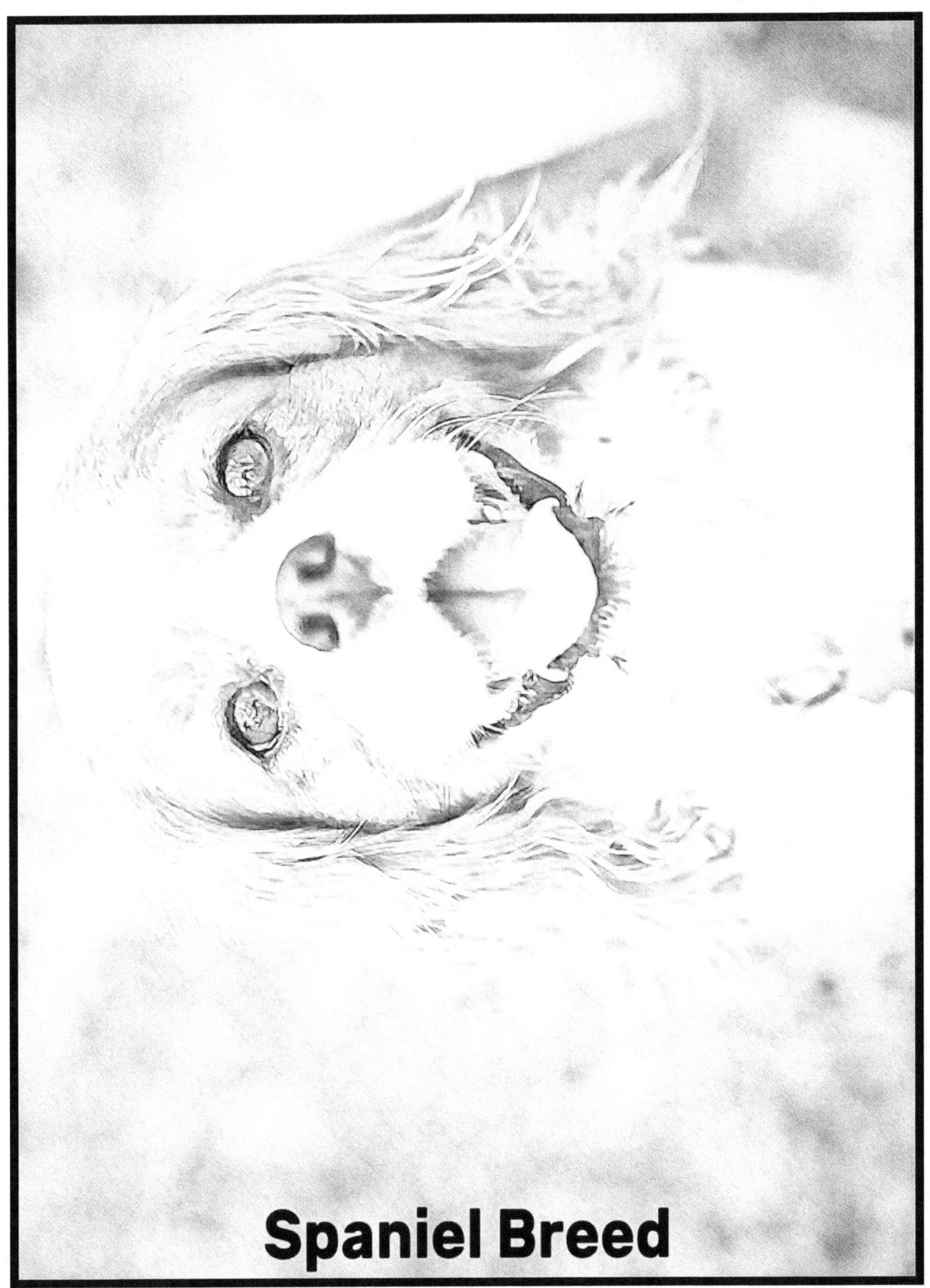

Spaniel Breed

Cesky Terrier Dog

Cocker Spaniel

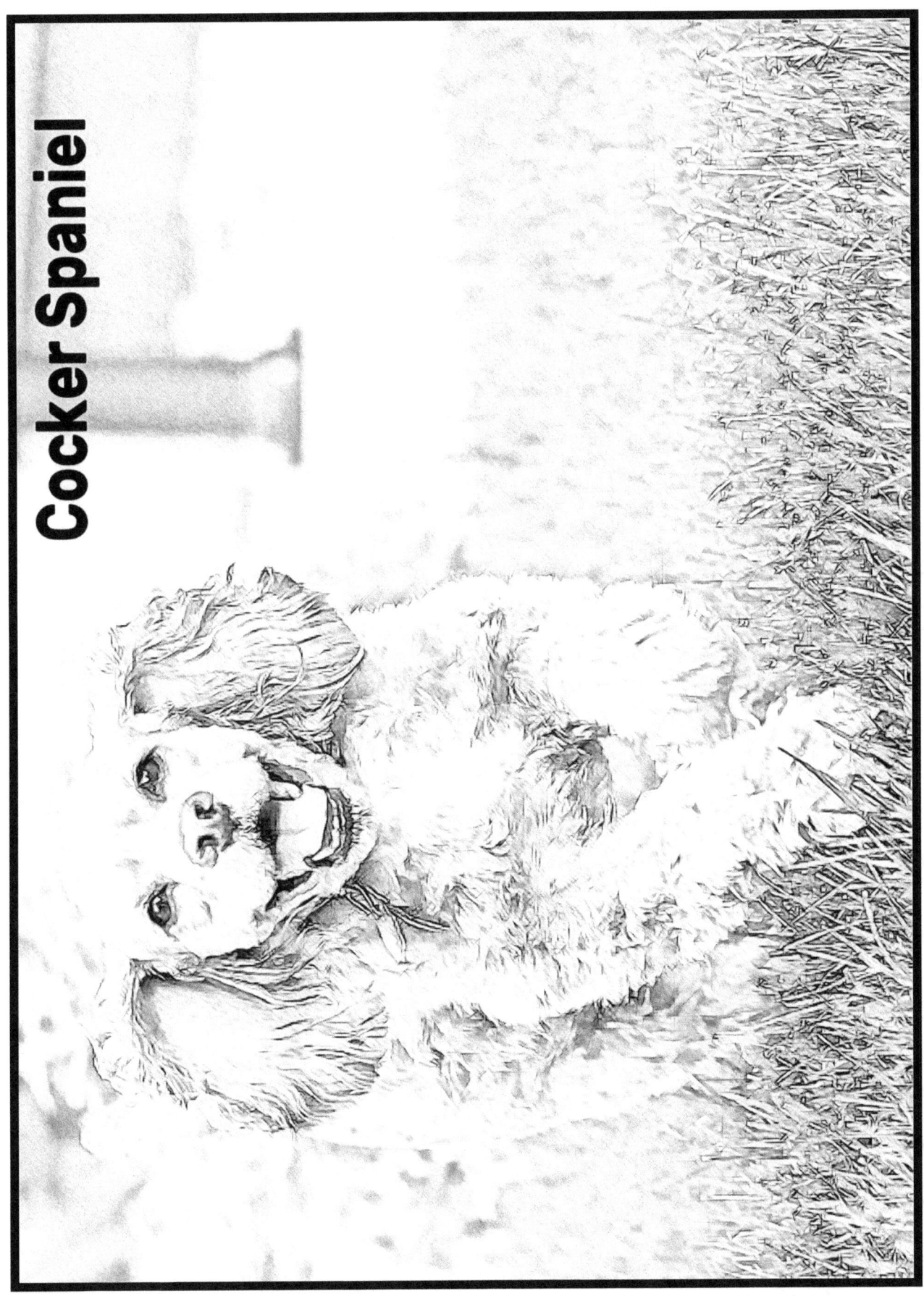

Corgi Breed

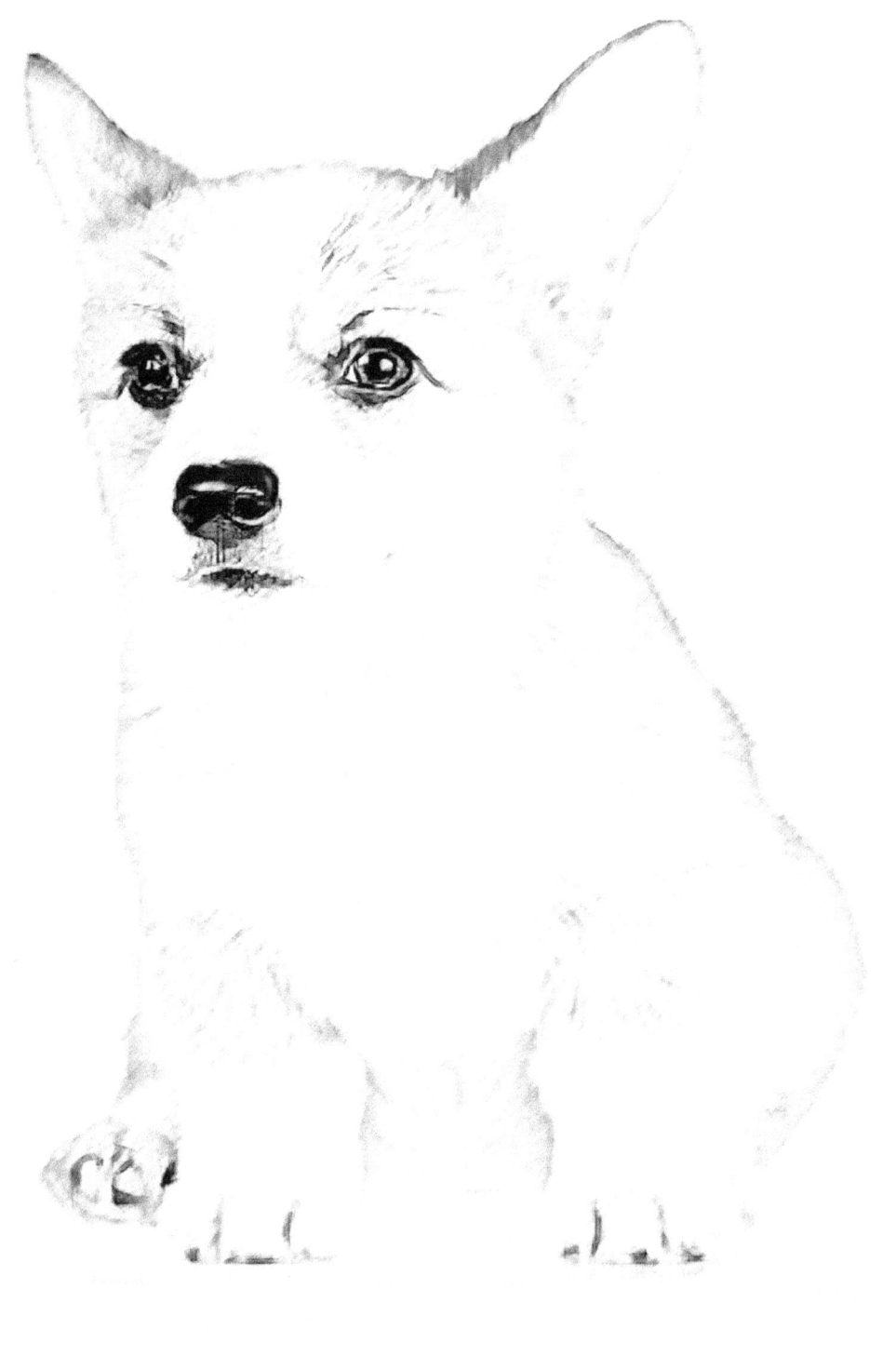

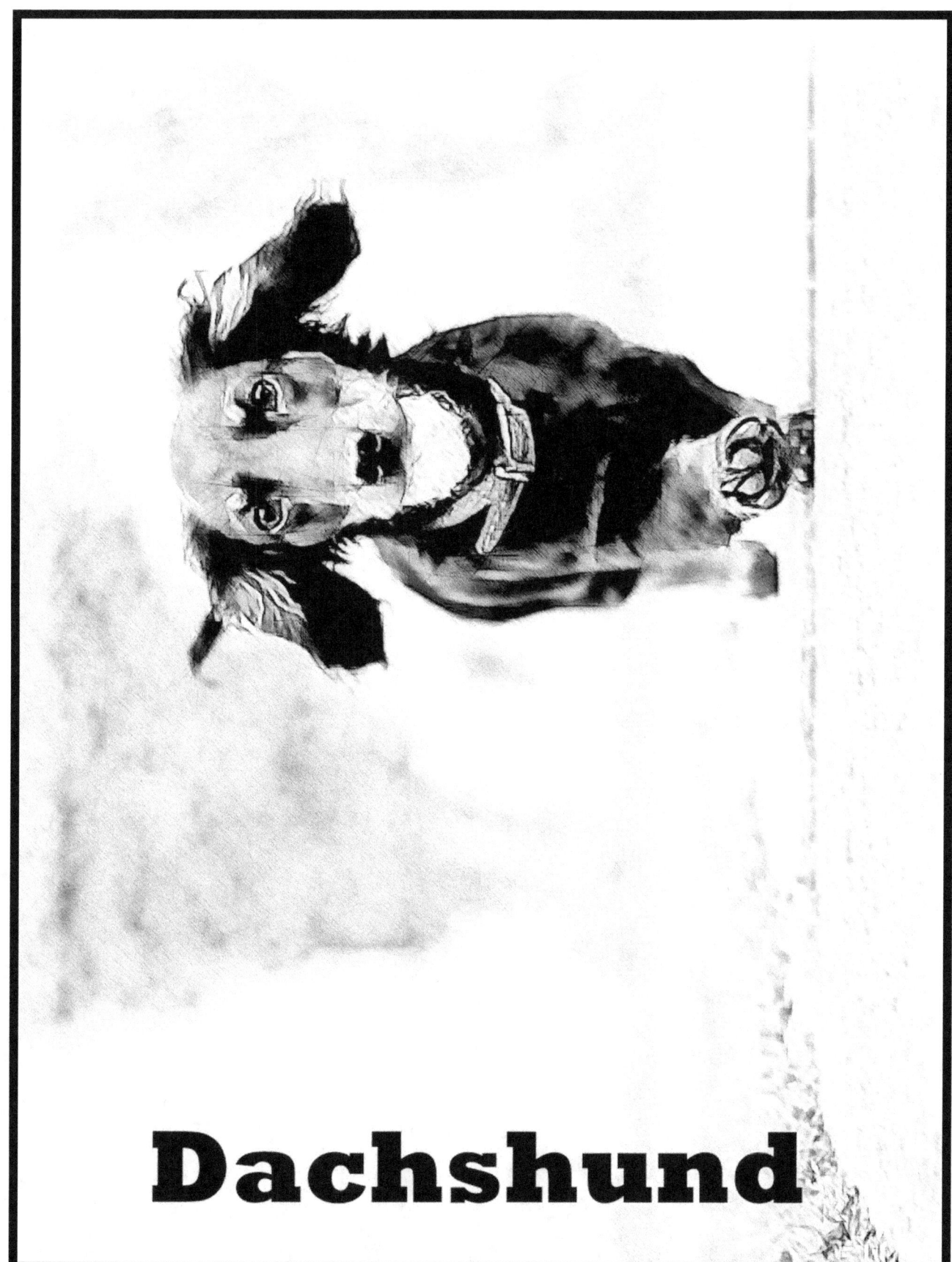

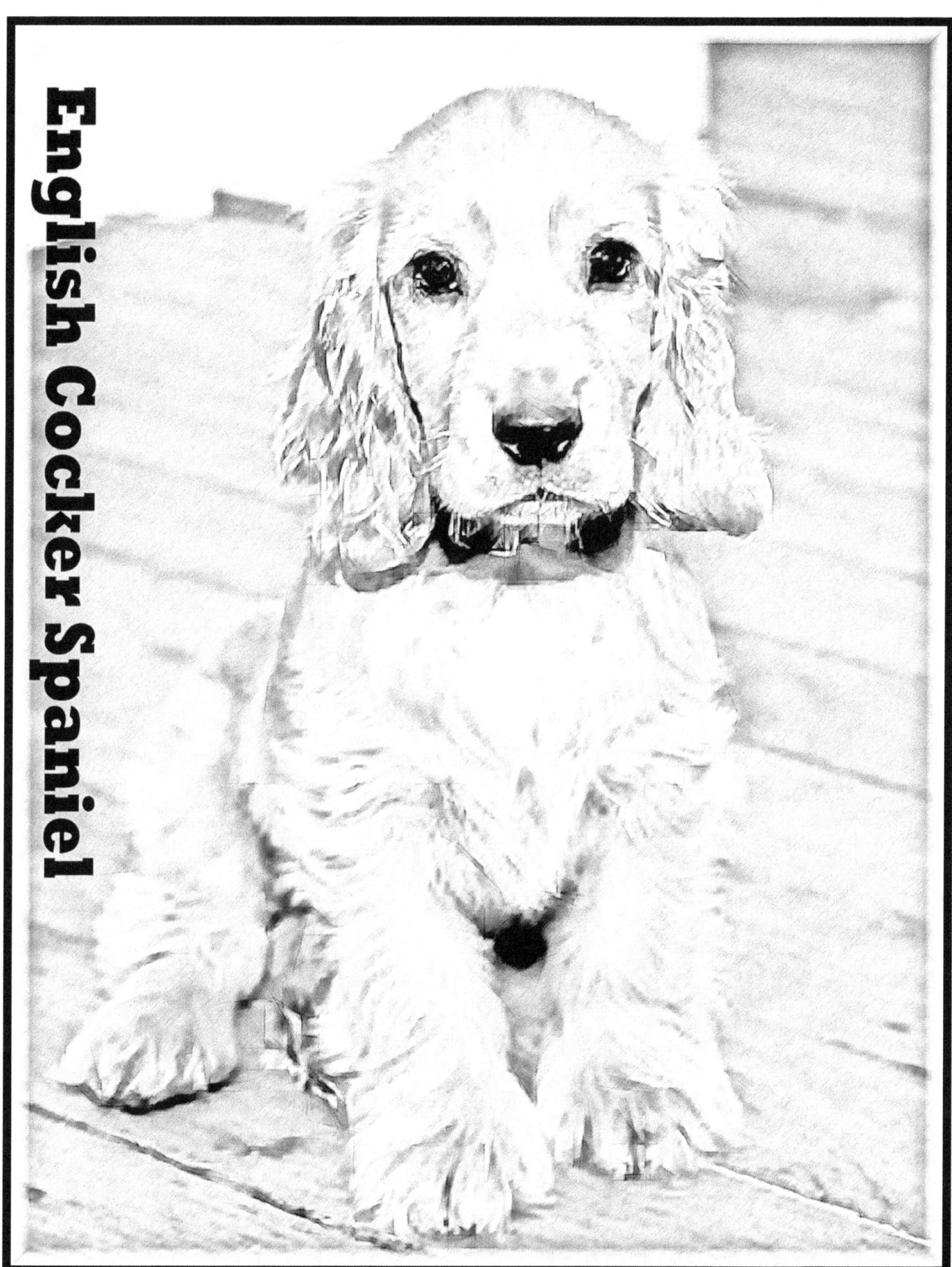

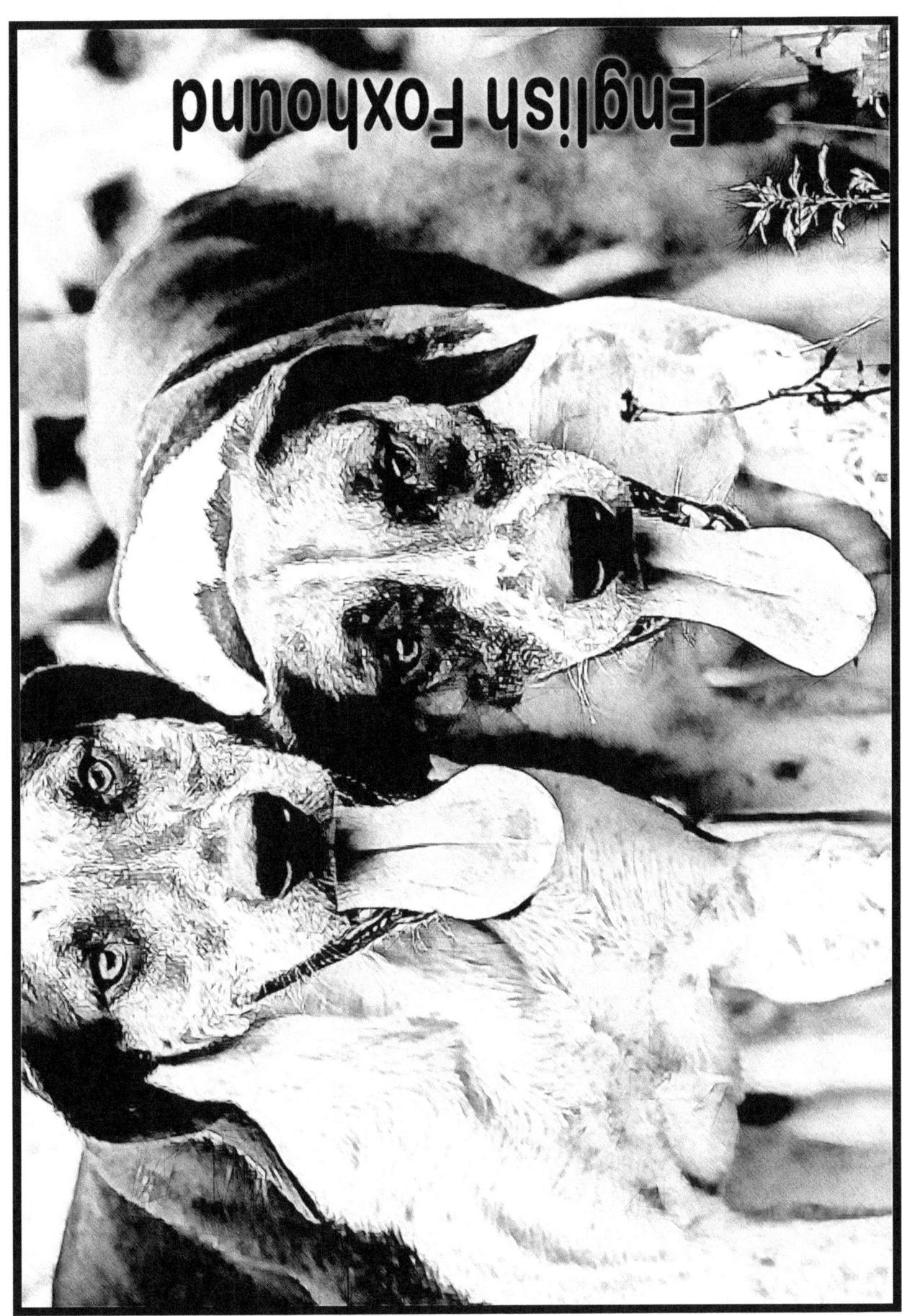

English Springer Spaniel

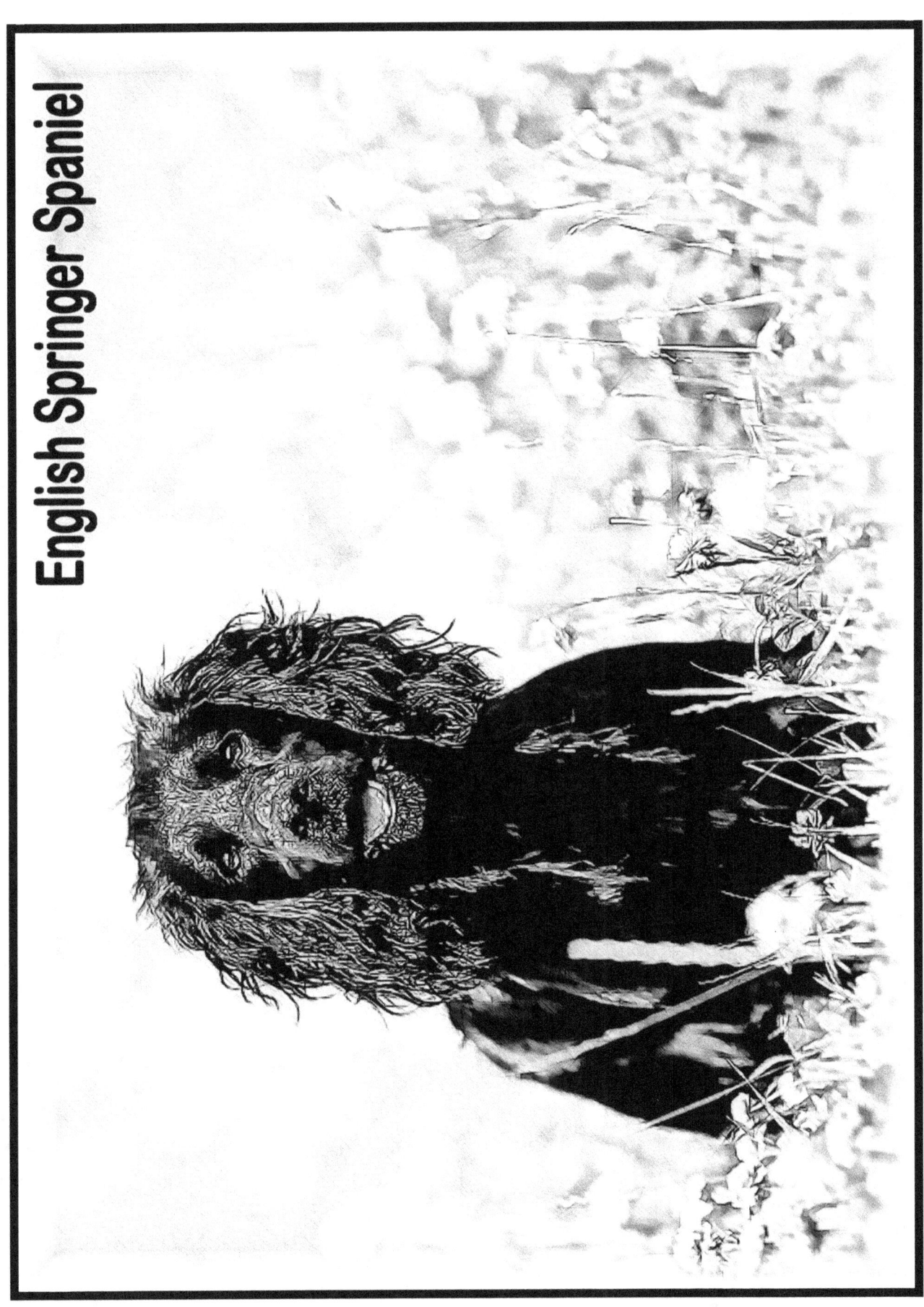

French Bulldog

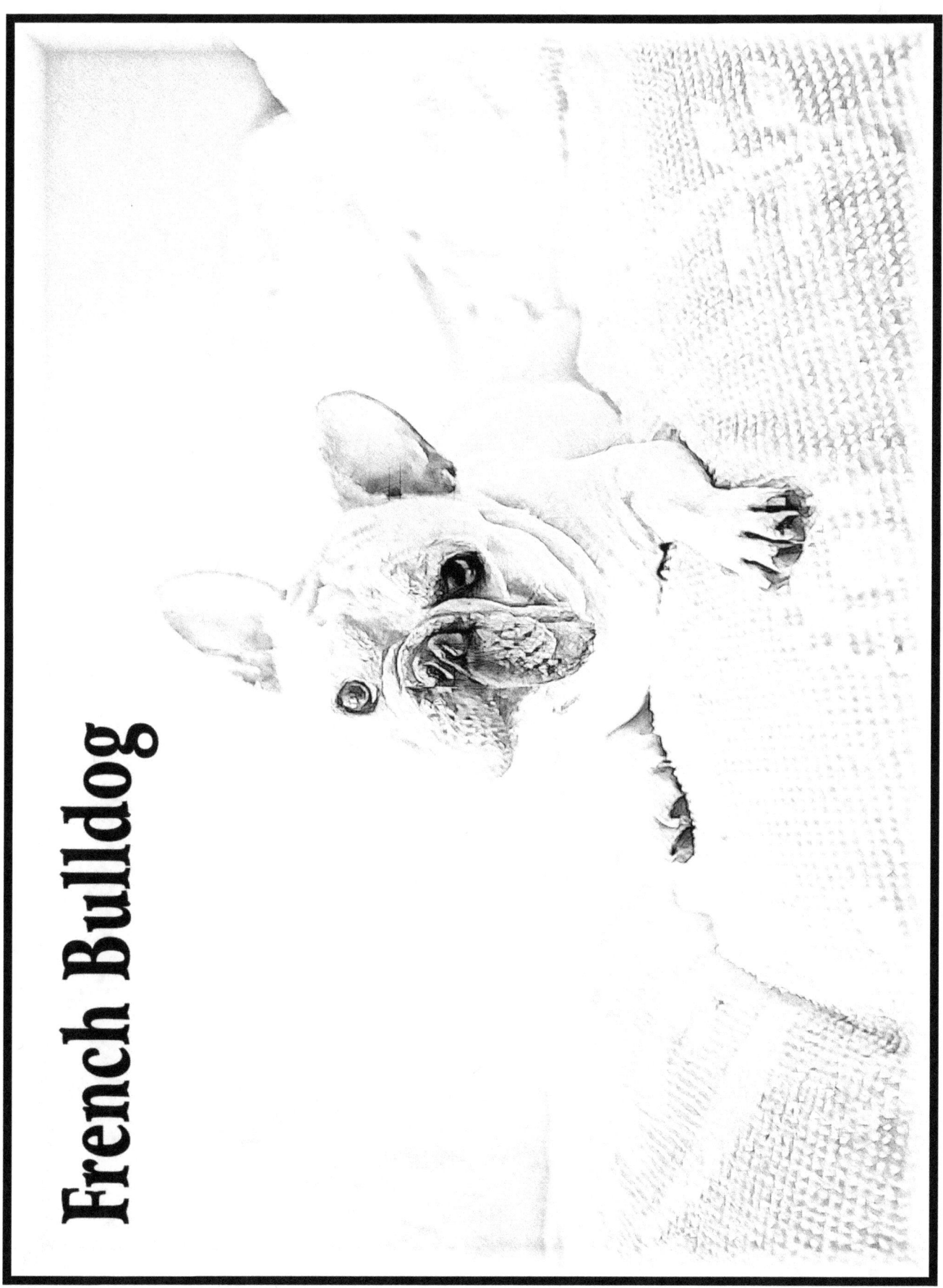

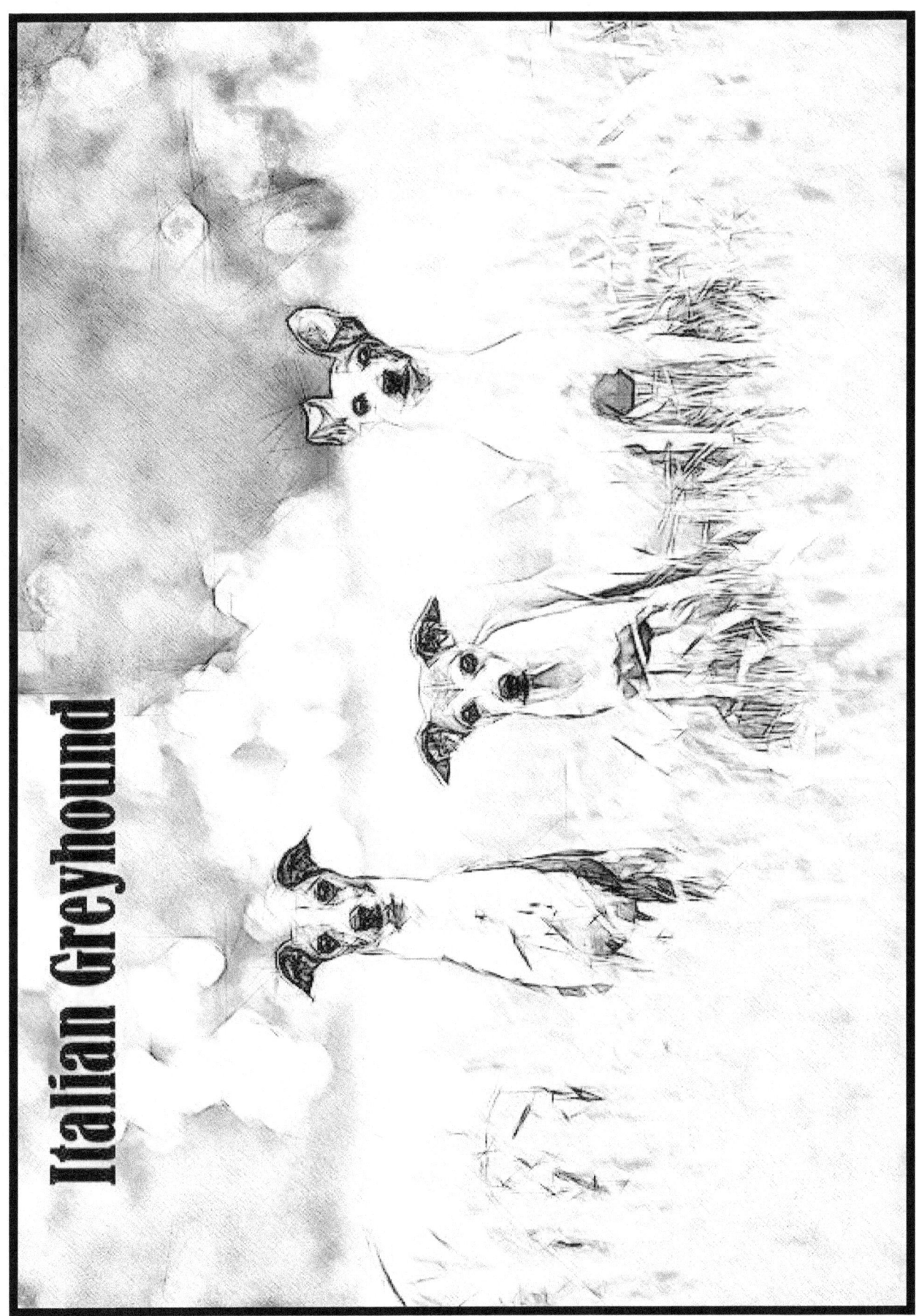
Italian Greyhound

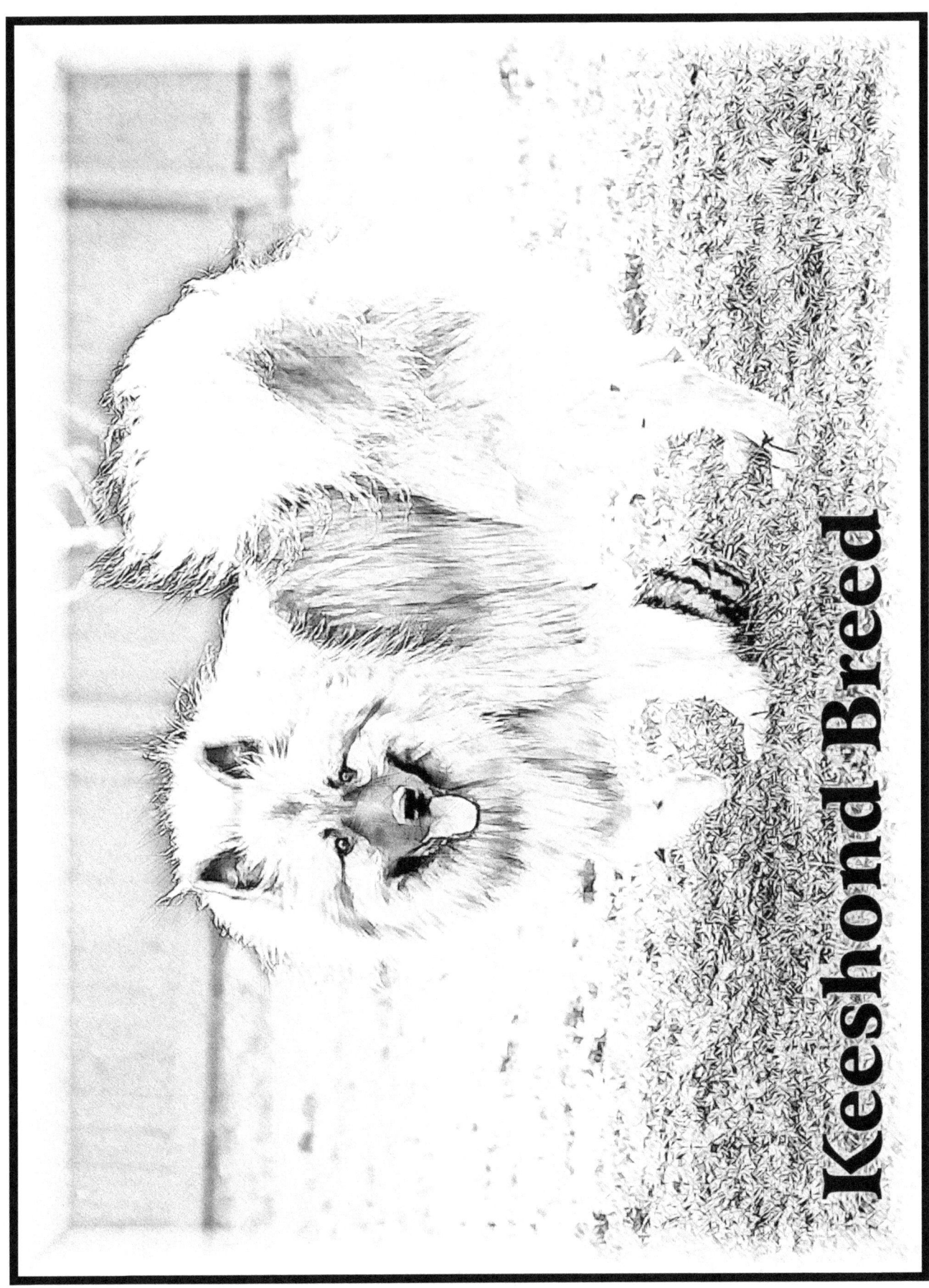

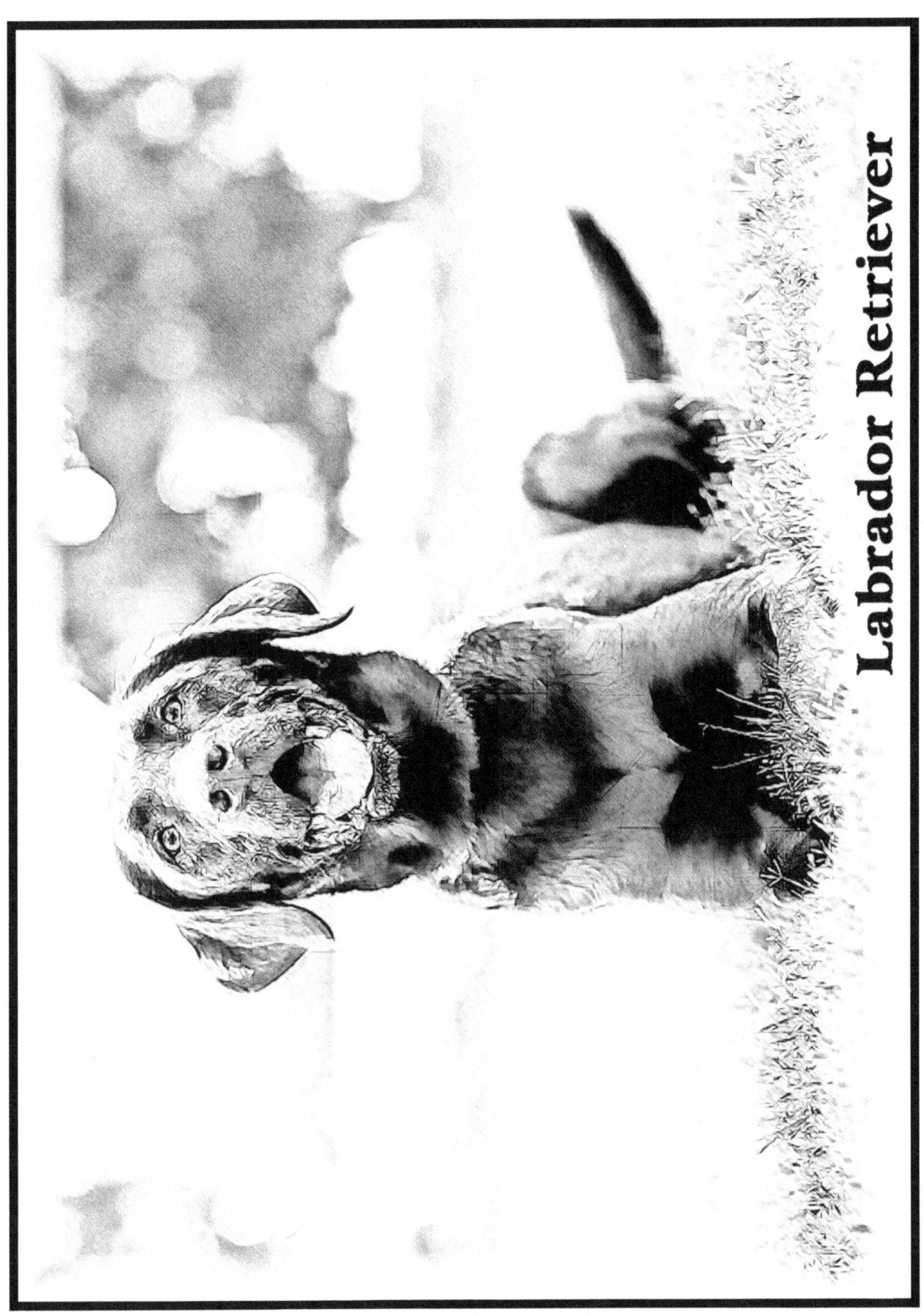

Labrador Retriever

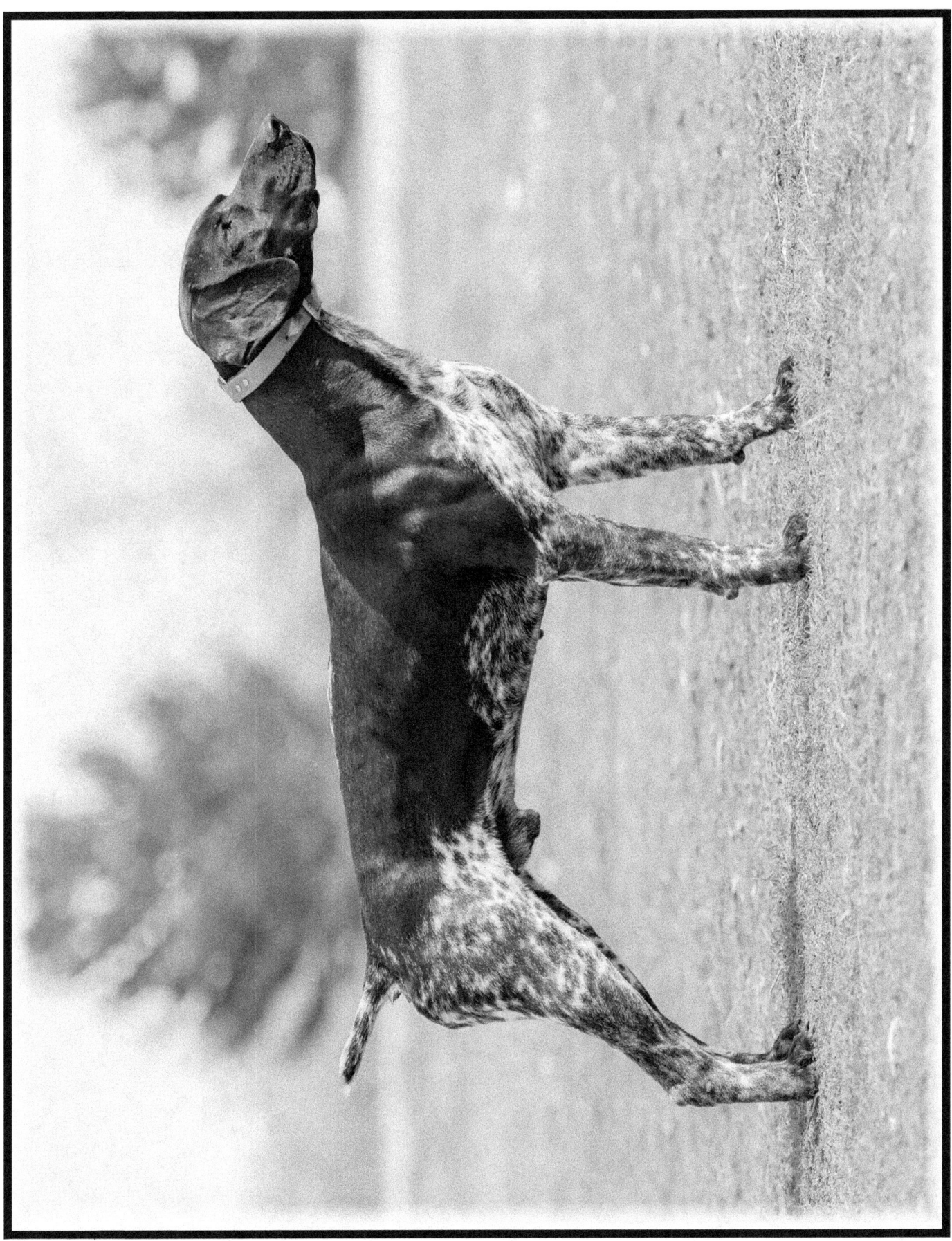

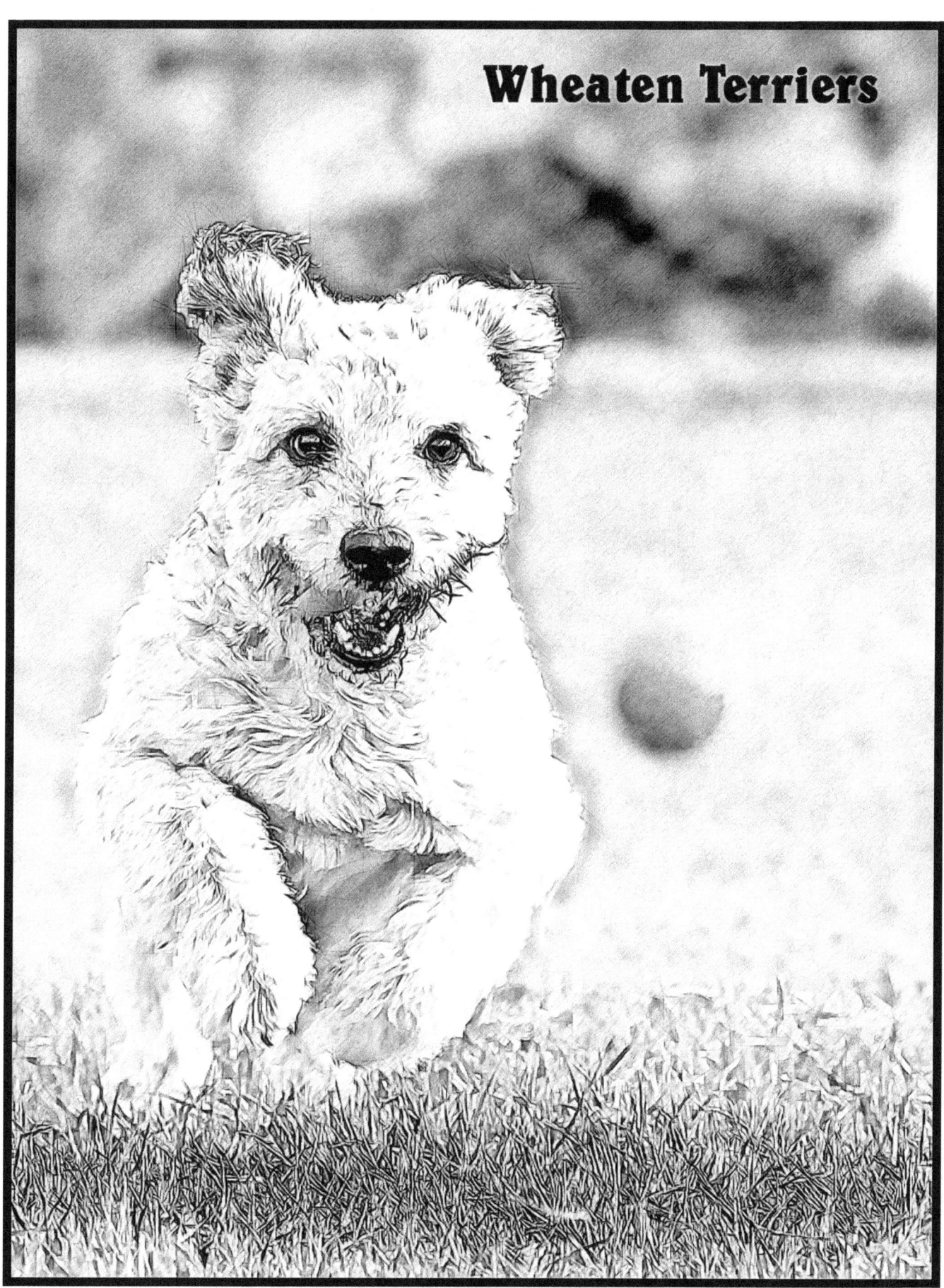

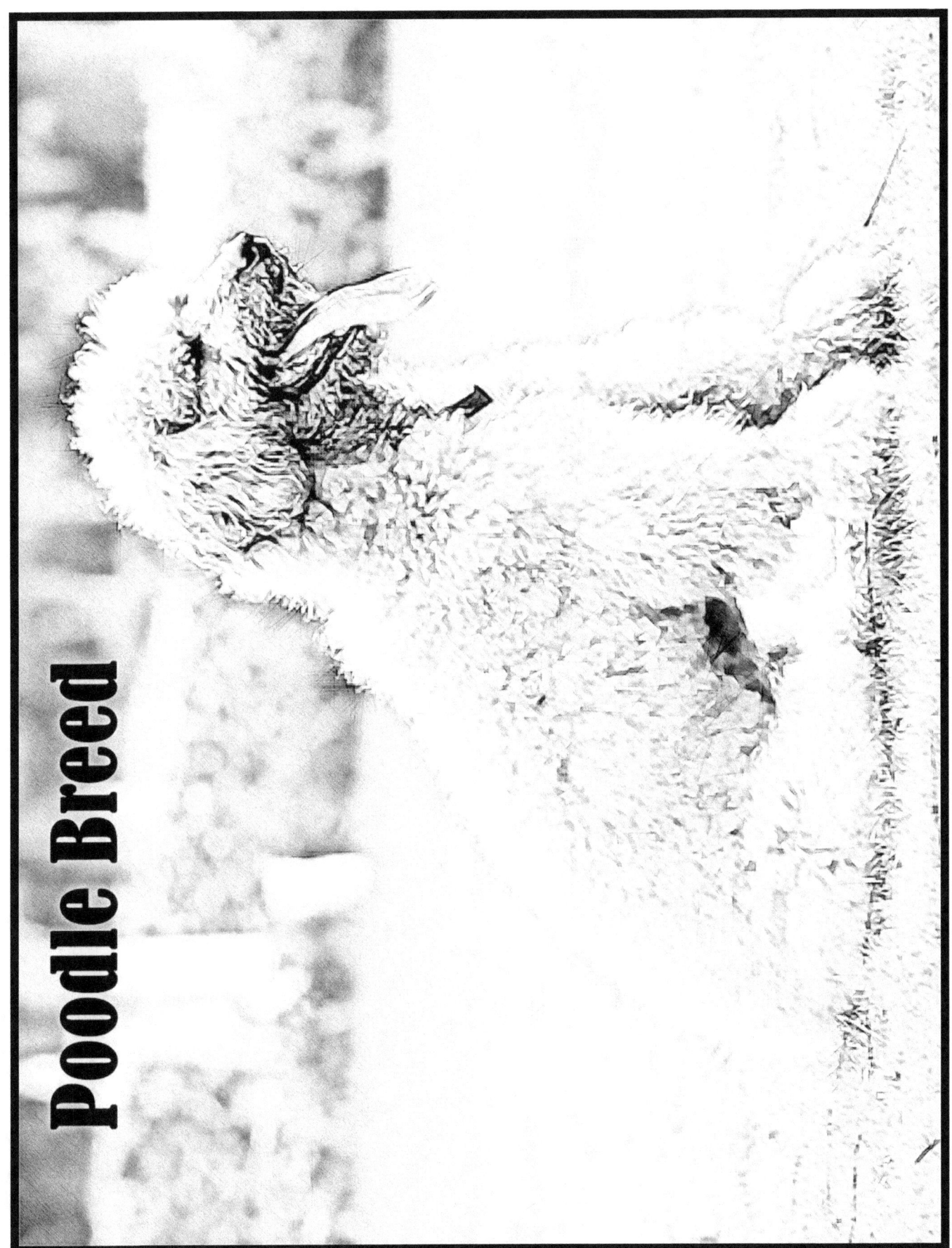

Poodle Breed

Portuguese Water Dogs

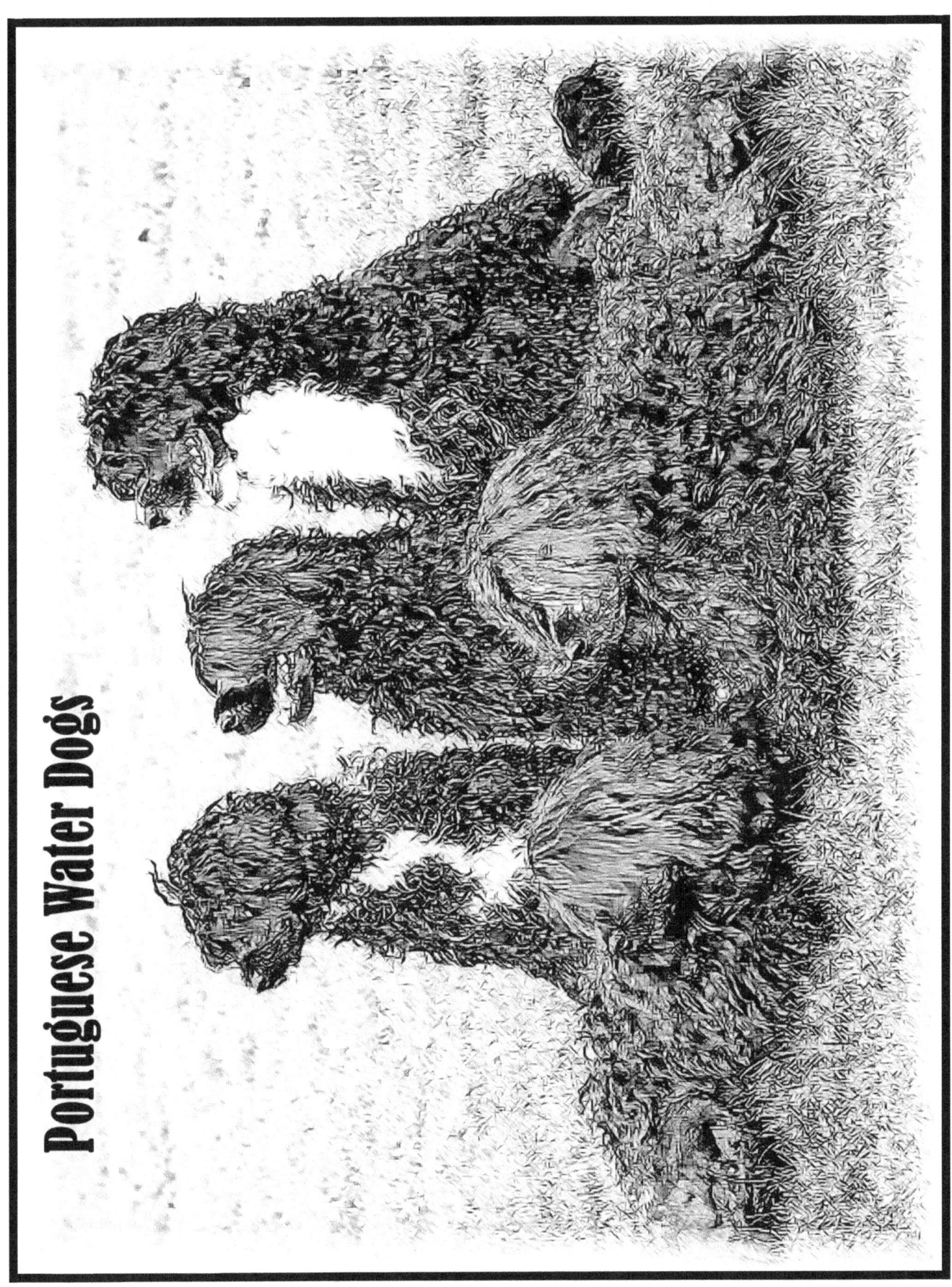

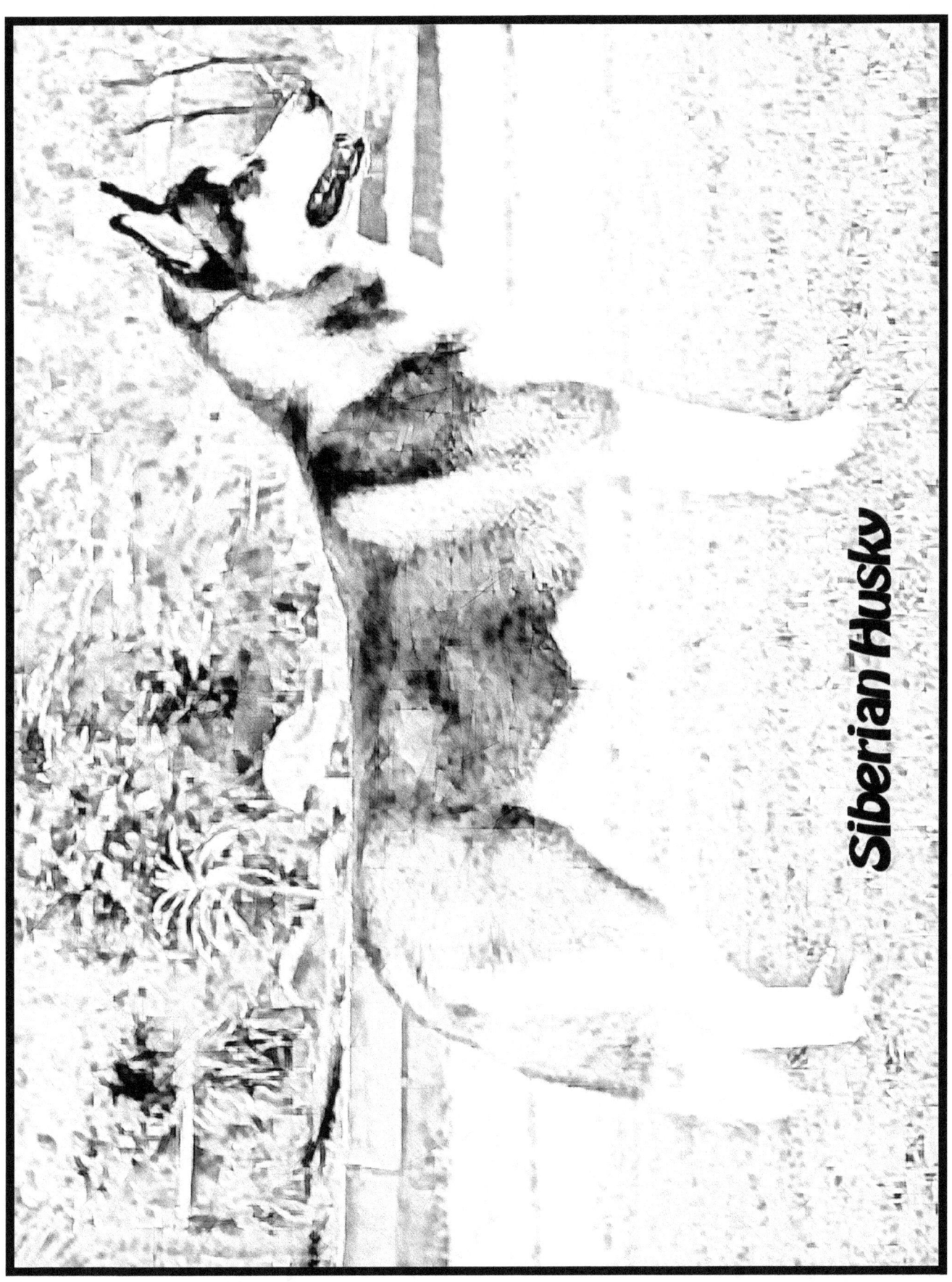

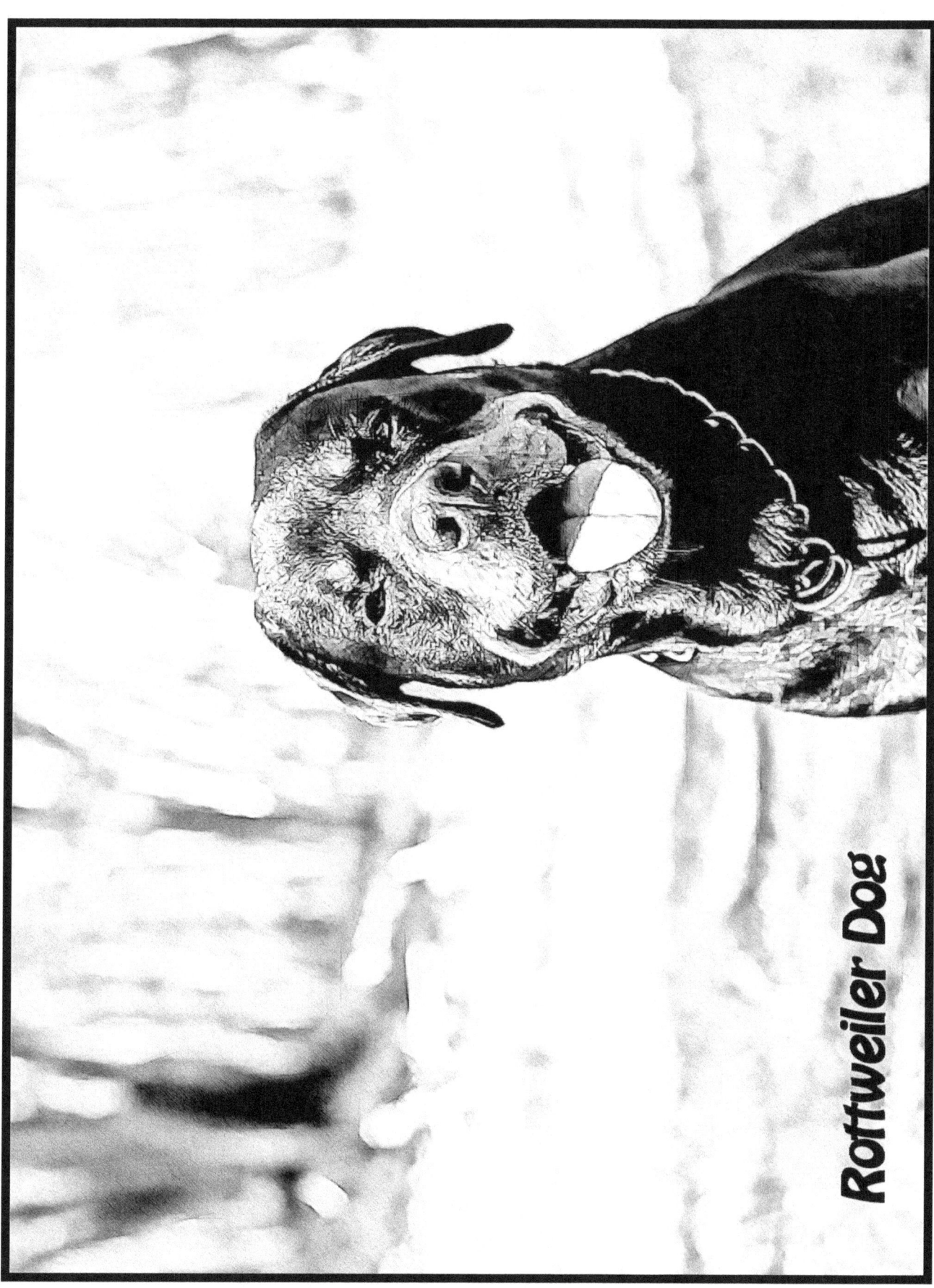

Rottweiler Dog

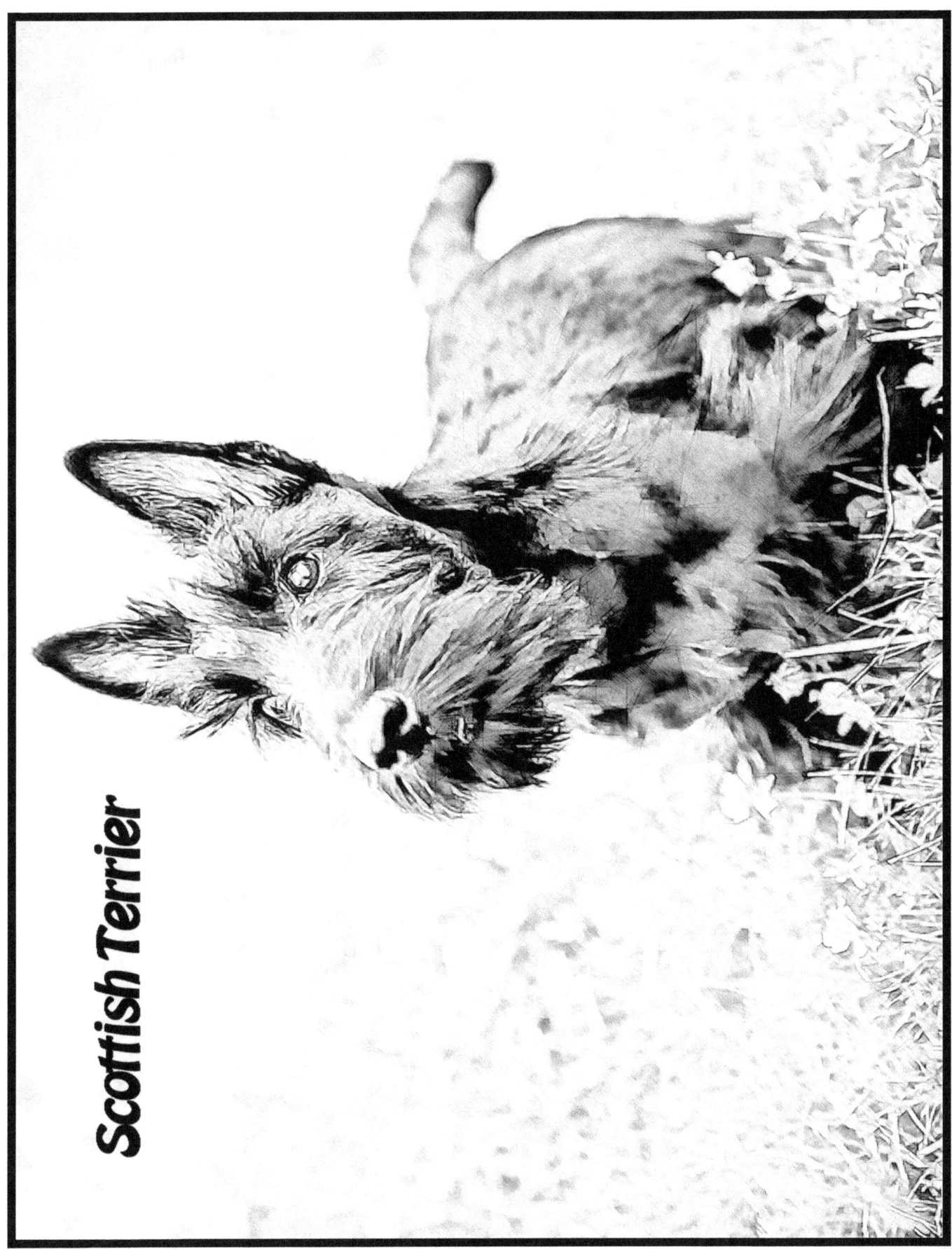

Scottish Terrier

Shar-Pei Breed

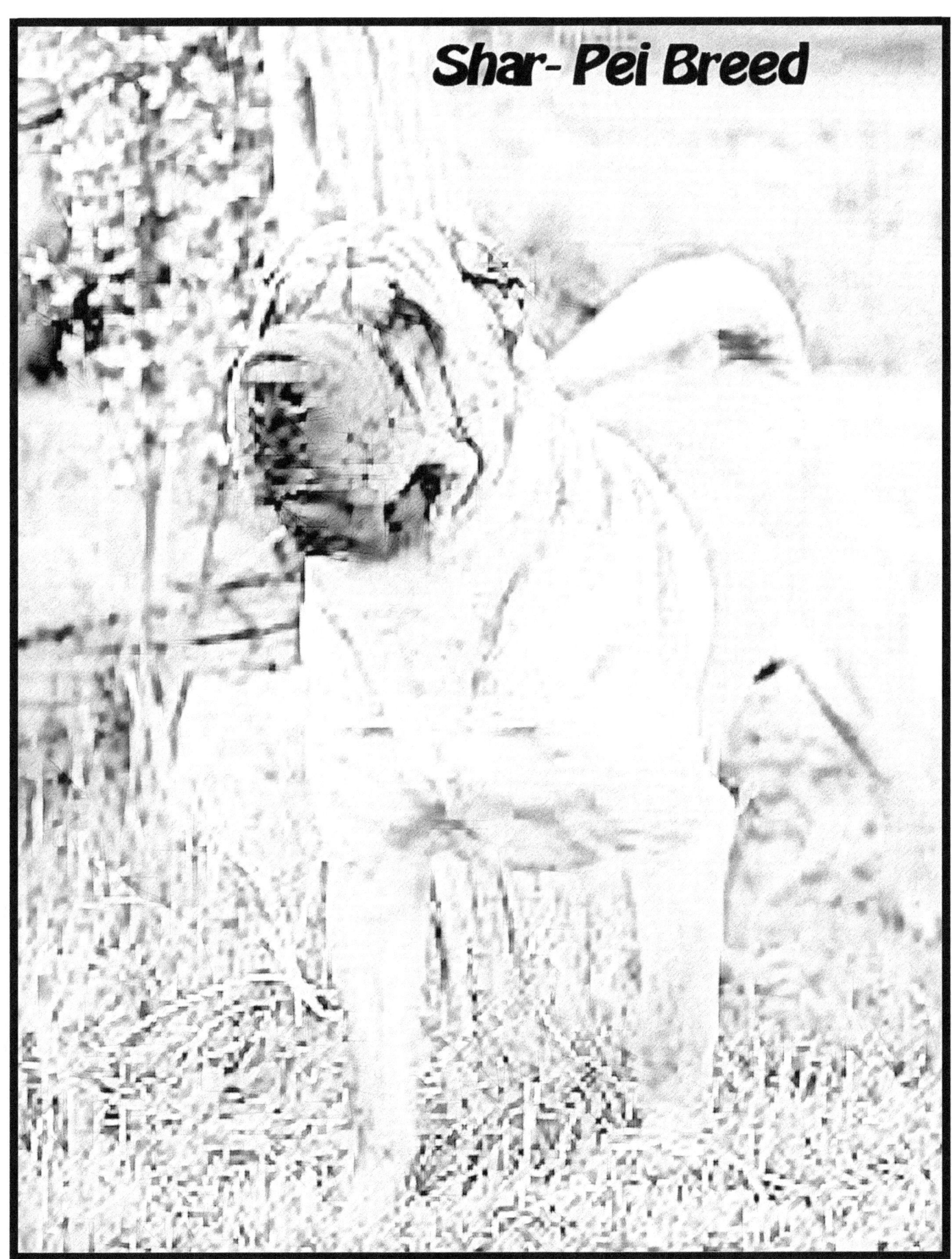

Shar-Pei Breed

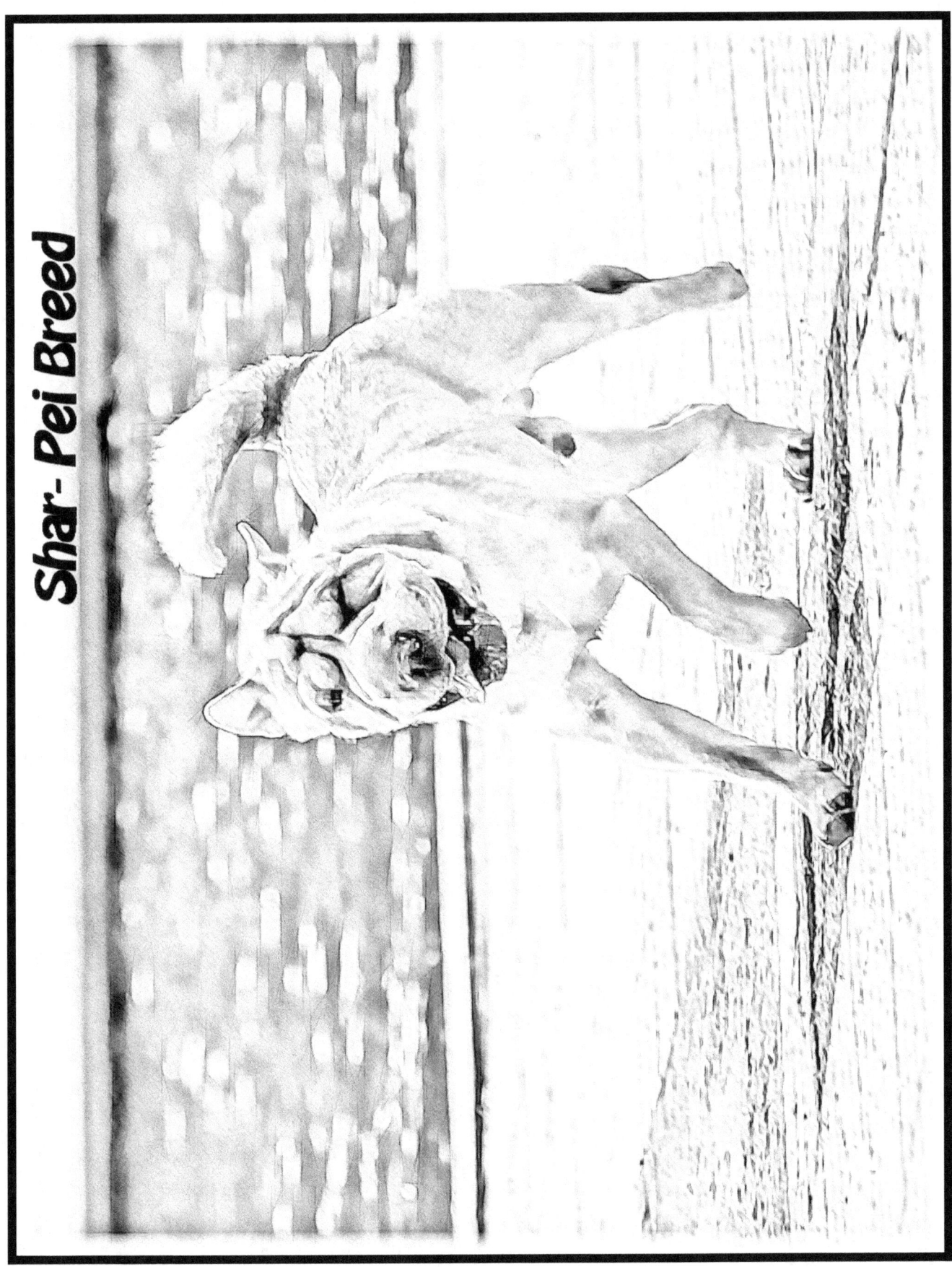

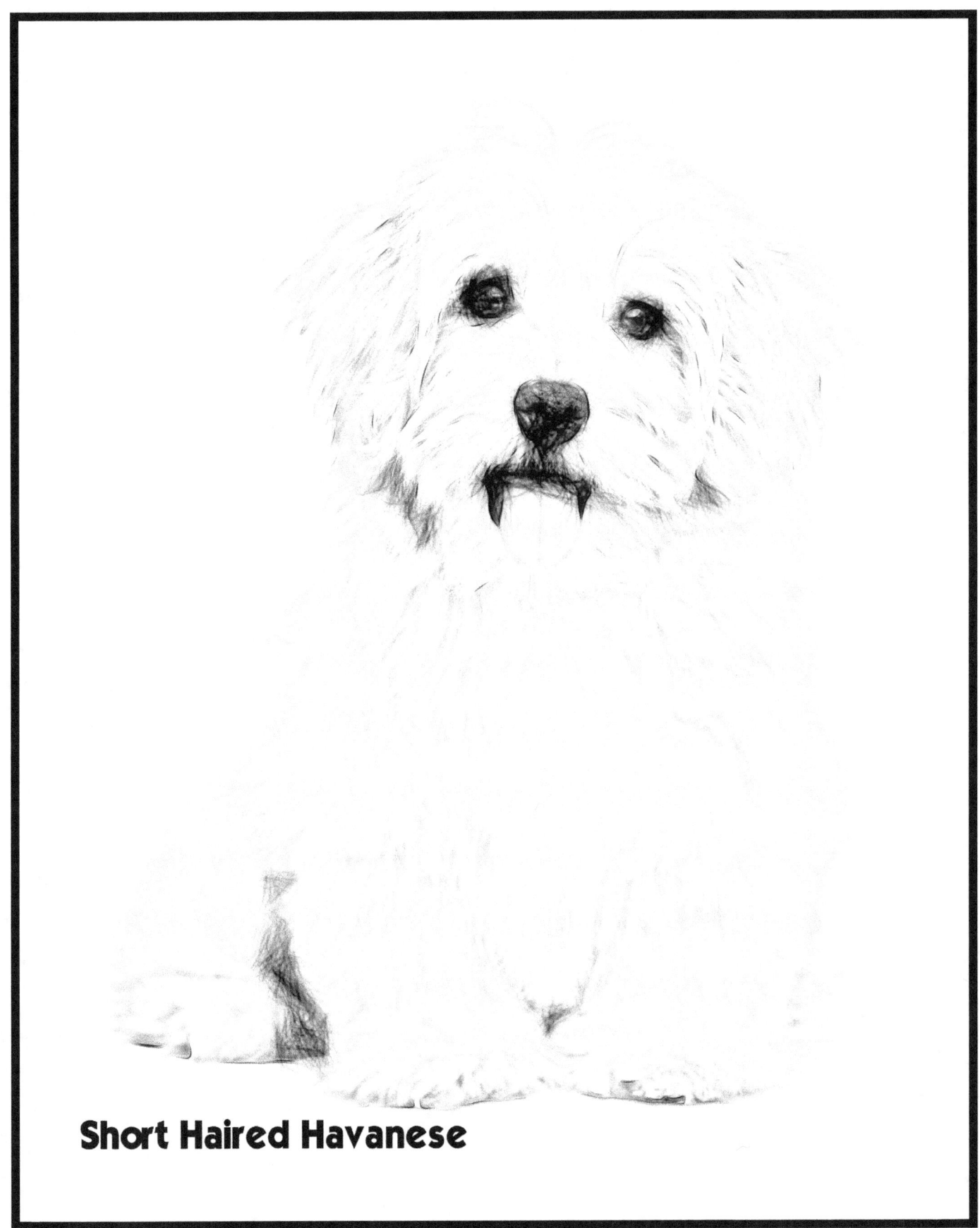

Short Haired Havanese

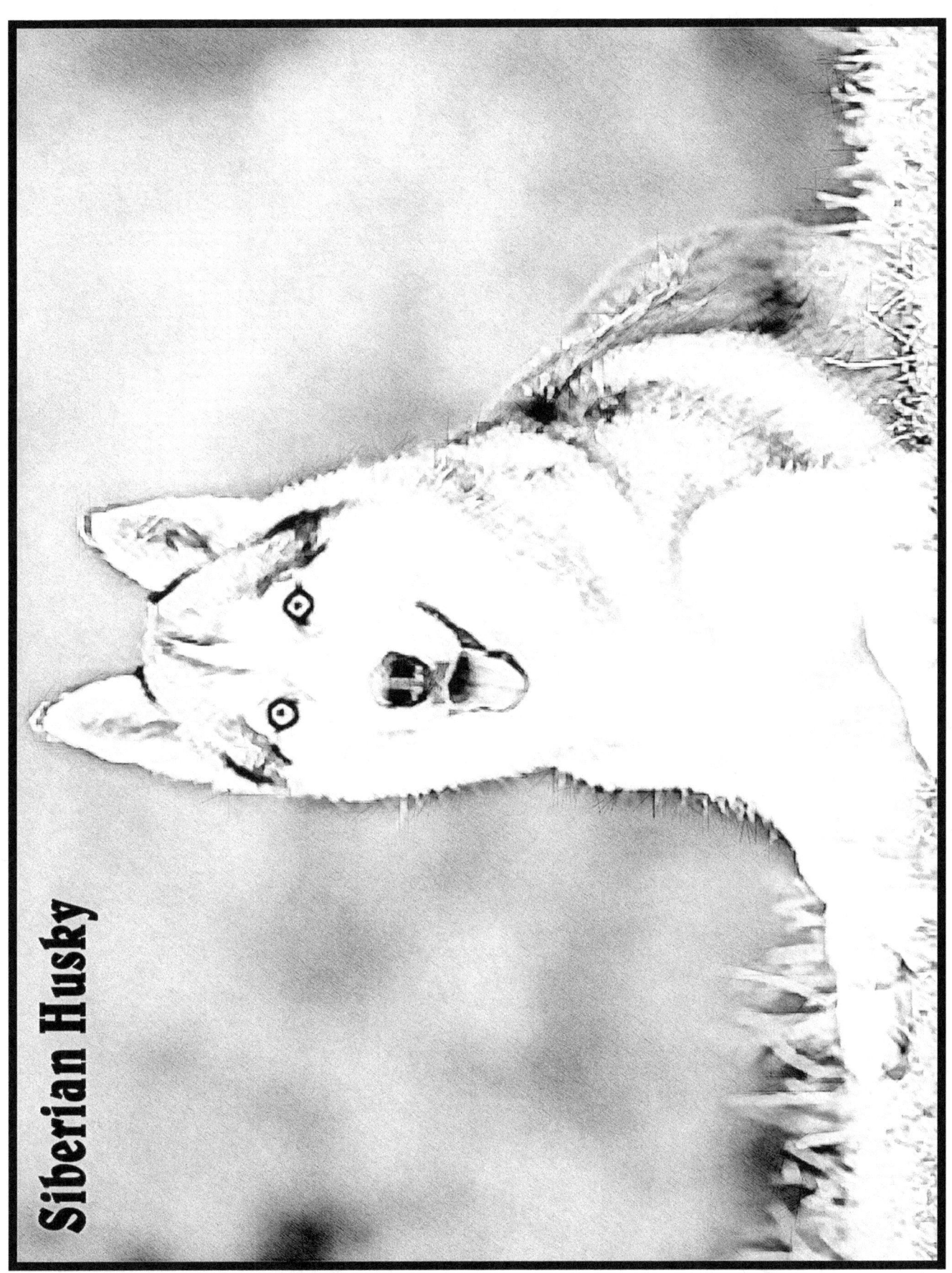
Siberian Husky

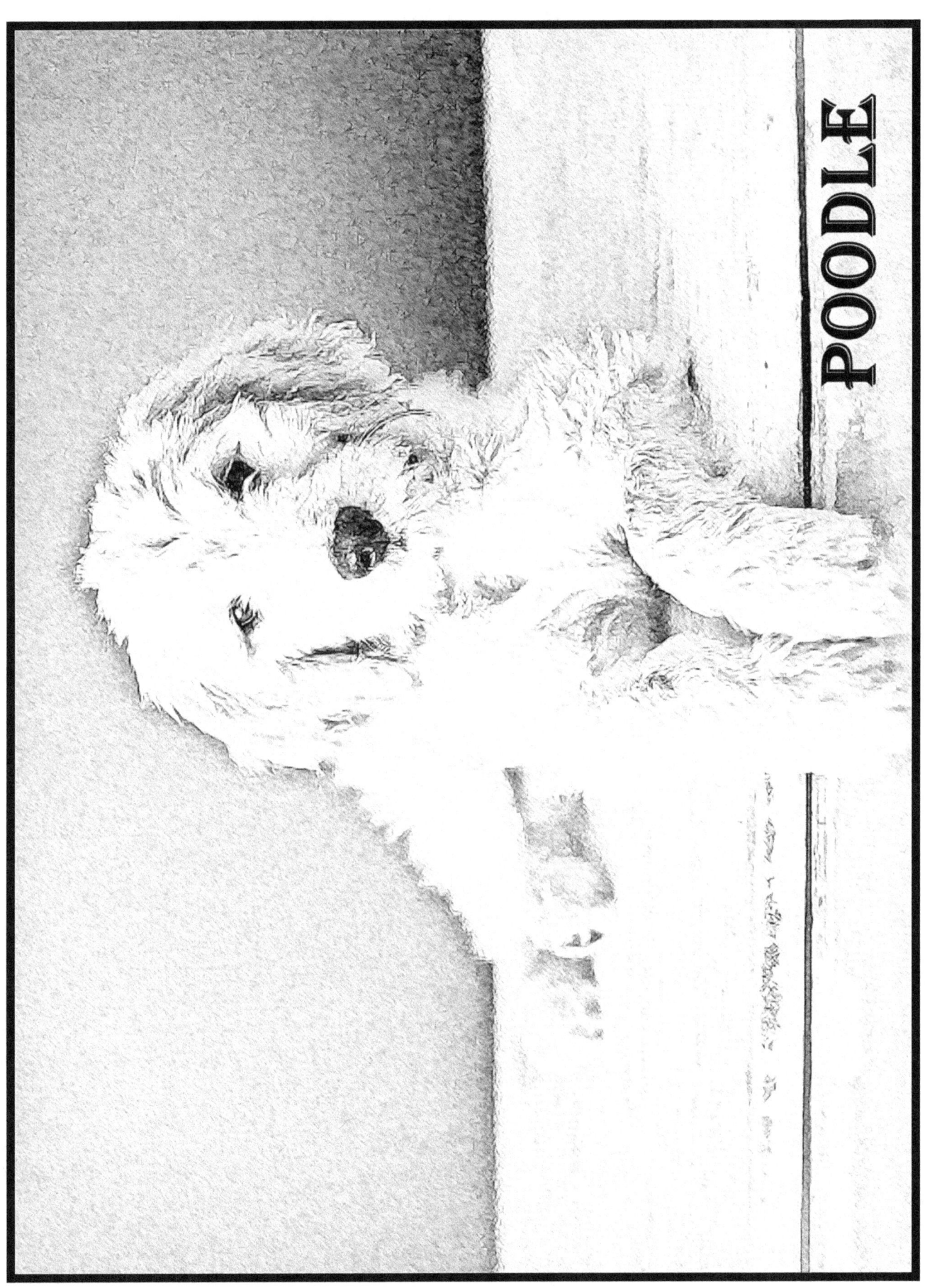

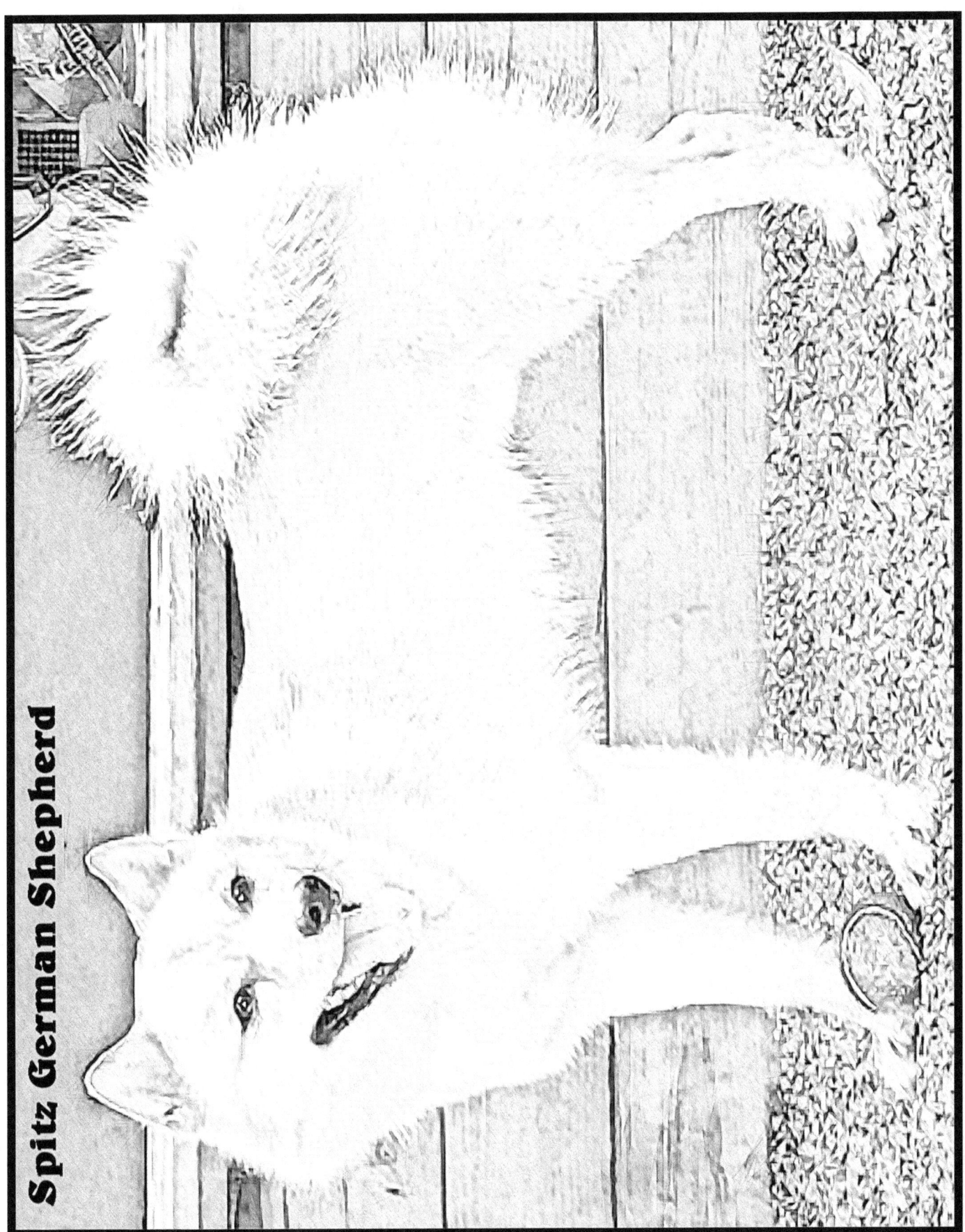

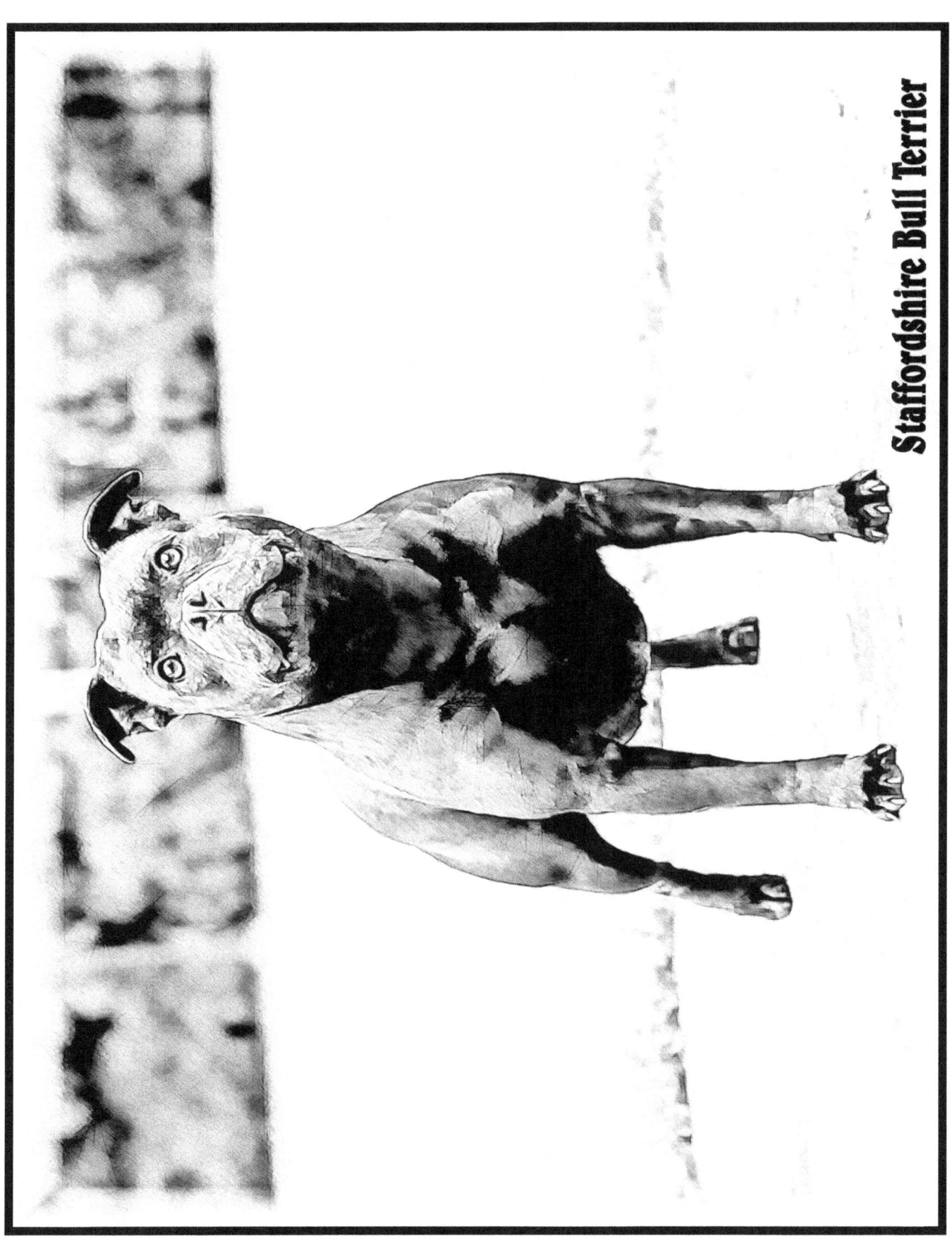

Staffordshire Bull Terrier

Welsh Corgi Dog

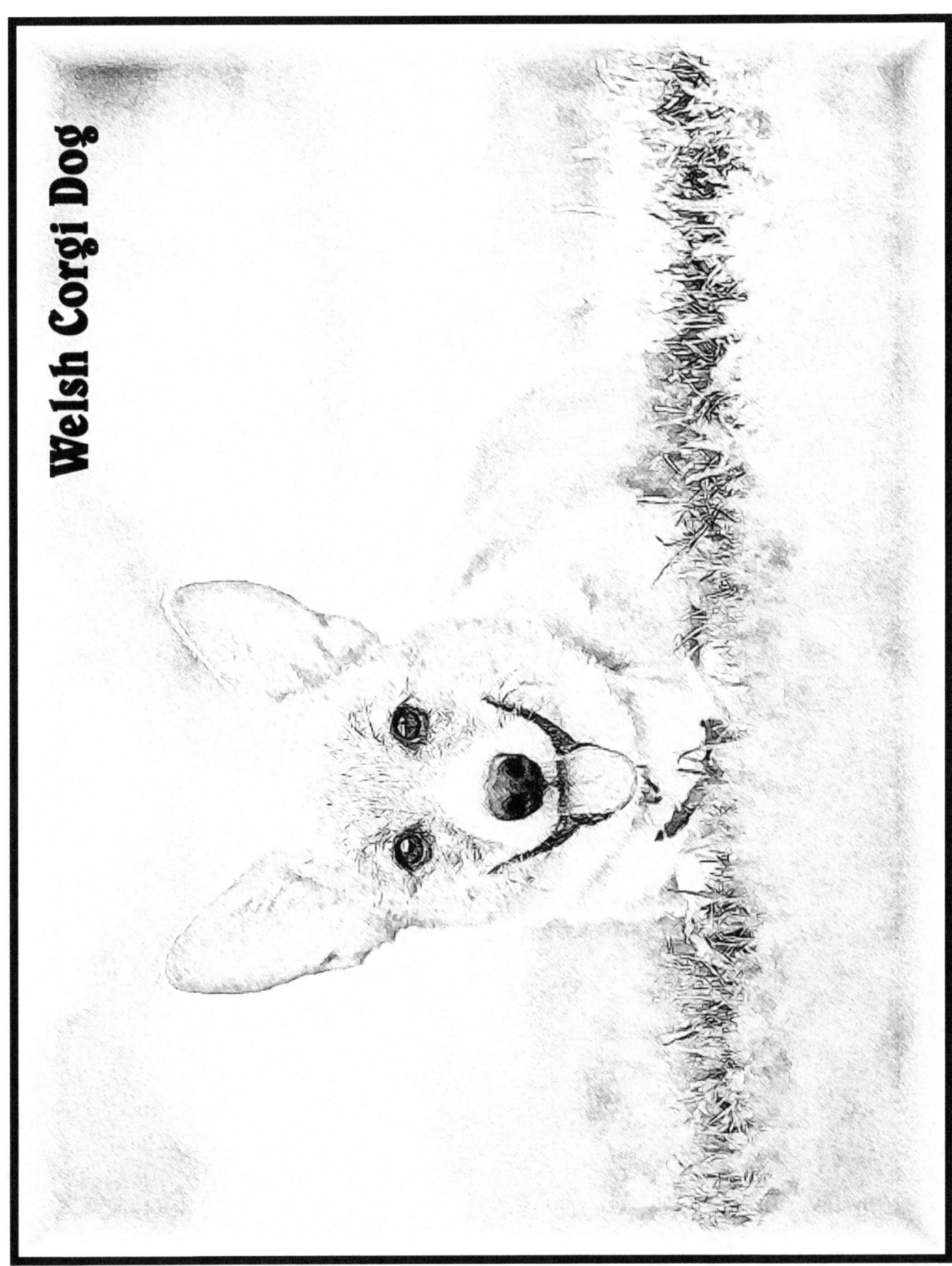

www.ingramcontent.com/pod-product-compliance
Lightning Source LLC
Chambersburg PA
CBHW081435220526
45466CB00008B/2391